KEY MA

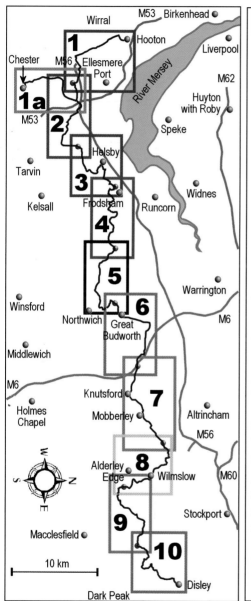

North Cheshire Way: The colour-coded key map on the left shows the eleven sections corresponding to the eleven chapters of the main part of this guide. Each chapter contains two route maps, with walking instructions. These outline maps are to scale and are up-to-date at the time of writing … and the entire route is waymarked. However, walkers are strongly encouraged to use the Ordnance Survey's 1:25000 scale "Explorer" maps for more detailed information. The maps numbered 266, 267 and 268 cover almost the entire route … with a tiny part at the eastern end falling onto "Explorer" map number OL1.

Notes:

1. On all the maps in this book north is either at the top or on the right; look for the compass rose.

2. Each map also has a scale indicator – 10 km on the key map, 1 km on all of the other maps. Remember that:

1 mile = about 1.6 km

1 km = about 0.6 miles

Key to Maps

ROADS AND PATHS

Motorways, A and B roads

Other motor roads

Paths and tracks
(not necessarily rights of way)

North Cheshire Way
(markers at 1 km intervals from west)

RAILWAYS

Railway

Tunnel

RIVERS AND CANALS

SYMBOLS

(2) Key point – *indicated in text by superscript*

Railway station   Public House

Point of interest

AREA FEATURES

Woodland   Lakes and reservoirs

The North Cheshire Way

"a slice of Cheshire"

A walker's guide to
Cheshire's longest footpath

The Mid-Cheshire Footpath Society

Published by The Mid-Cheshire Footpath Society – www.mcfs.org.uk.

Copyright © The Mid-Cheshire Footpath Society

ISBN 0-9553573-0-6 (old format)

ISBN 978-0-9553573-0-5 (new format)

Disclaimer

The contents of this book are believed to be correct at the time of printing. Nevertheless, the publishers cannot be held responsible for any errors or omissions or for any changes in the details given in this book or for any consequences of any reliance on the information it provides. We have tried to ensure accuracy in this book, but footpaths do change. We would be grateful if readers advise us of any inaccuracies they may encounter. This does not affect your statutory rights. We have taken all reasonable steps to ensure that this route should be safe to walk and achievable by walkers with a realistic level of fitness. However, all outdoor activities involve a degree of risk and the publishers accept no responsibility for any injuries arising from walking the North Cheshire Way. For more advice, see page 5.

Acknowledgments

The Mid-Cheshire Footpath Society gratefully acknowledges:

o   Financial support provided towards the publication of this book by: Cestrian Ramblers Group, Cheshire County Council, F H Properties Ltd. (Frank Hockenhull and David Vernon), Macclesfield Borough Council, Mersey Forest (supported by Linley, Wightman, Shaw Foundation), the Ramblers Association and Vale Royal Borough Council.

o   The efforts of many of its members in researching, surveying and waymarking the North Cheshire Way and in writing, designing and illustrating this book.

o   The inspiration of the late David Kinsell – footpath walker and friend – whose idea this was, but who did not live to see it come to fruition.

CONTENTS

INTRODUCTION

THE NORTH CHESHIRE WAY

USEFUL INFORMATION

HOW TO USE THIS BOOK

This book is a walker's guide to the North Cheshire Way. Opened in 2006 as Cheshire's longest long-distance footpath, this runs from Wirral in the west to the Dark Peak in the east. The complete route is 114 km (71 miles) long, but it is well suited to walking in sections of any length from an afternoon stroll to a day's hike. The maps show nearby footpaths as well as the North Cheshire Way itself so that circular routes can be devised based on the main trail. Alternatively, it can be fun to walk with friends. By taking two cars and leaving one at each end of a section of the route, a linear walk is possible without retracing one's steps.

The introductory section of the book provides background information on the route. The final section of the book provides references to practical information on transport, accommodation, refreshment and places of interest. It also gives some background on The Mid-Cheshire Footpath Society, who created the North Cheshire Way, and their other named and waymarked trails in Cheshire. The main part of the book is divided into eleven chapters – chapters 1-10 for the main line of the North Cheshire Way from Hooton station in the west to Disley station in the east, and an additional chapter 1a for the spur route from Chester station that joins the main line on the Shropshire Union Canal at Croughton. Each chapter covers a distance of about 5 – 6 km (3 – 4 miles) along the route. The frontispiece to the book provides an overview map that gives a key to the areas covered by the individual chapters.

Each chapter has two maps and, on the facing pages, detailed walking directions for the mapped sections of the route. The walking instructions are laid out in two columns – one for each direction, west-to-east and east-to-west. The rest of each chapter describes the landscape, natural, human and industrial history for the section – together with a brief indication of other points of interest along the route or nearby. This narrative is written from the perspective of a walker going from west to east, but is in short sections so should be easy to use in the reverse direction. We've included some pictures, some anecdotes and – for "foreigners" – a little Cheshire vocabulary.

The maps are oriented with north either at the top or on the right – take note of the compass rose on each map. The maps are to scale – take note of the 1 km (1100 yards) scale on each map. There is a key to map symbols on the reverse side of the frontispiece of the book. Superscript numbers in the walking instructions link to corresponding circled numbers on the maps. The maps show the route with nearby roads, paths and points of interest. Pubs are included in rural areas (but, for reasons of space, not in the larger centres of population, which may be assumed to be well provided with such hostelries).

HOW TO WALK THE PATH

Waymarks and Maps: The entire route has been waymarked by The Mid-Cheshire Footpath Society. The waymarks are circular and show a yellow directional arrow on a black background; the arrow is marked with the letters "NCW". In theory, it should be possible to walk the path by waymarks alone. However, this is not advised, as things can change and waymarks do have a habit of "disappearing". The walking instructions and sectional maps in this book provide a lot more detail and should suffice for most purposes. However, it is always possible that you may encounter difficulties, wish to return by a different route or need to access a nearby road or village in case of an emergency. We therefore strongly recommend that walkers purchase and carry the relevant Ordnance Survey map(s). The "Explorer" series maps are the best for walkers. They are printed at a scale of 1:25000 (1 cm on the map represents 250m on the ground, about 2½ inches to the mile) and show footpaths and roads, as well as the terrain right down to the level of individual field boundaries. See also "Navigation" on page 106.

It is also worth remembering that things change! Paths may be diverted, obstacles appear and signs get moved. We have tried very hard to make sure that the instructions in this book are accurate, clear and up-to-date at the time of publication. If you do find any difficulties or changes, we would very much like to hear from you. Contact The Mid-Cheshire Footpath Society (either via our web site at www.mcfs.org.uk or by e-mail to info@mcfs.org.uk). Alternatively, contact Cheshire County Council's Public Rights of Way Maintenance Unit at http://www.cheshire.gov.uk/countryside/Prow/ReportPathProblem.htm).

Terrain: The terrain is varied – field and woodland paths and tracks, riverside paths and canal towpaths, some quiet lanes and short sections of busier roads. There are short sections of higher-level hill and moorland tracks, but the path is not a high-level route; the maximum altitude is only 287m (941 ft).

Clothing and Footwear: Very little in the way of special equipment is needed for walking the path. However, a little common sense in choosing what to wear – especially on your feet – can make a very big difference to the enjoyment of a day out. Comfortable and waterproof boots that have been "walked in" are ideal in all weather – as for nearly all walking in England. In dry weather, reasonably heavy-duty trainers are perfectly adequate. Wellington boots are not recommended, as they tend to cause blisters. Socks should be cotton (nylon tends to cause blisters) and many walkers find that two pairs, one thin and one thicker, are better than one for comfort on longer walks. Other clothing should follow the principle that several layers are often better than one. This allows the walker to adjust to the temperature and wind chill – and two layers are always warmer than one layer at double the thickness. In cold weather, you will feel much warmer if you have gloves and a hat as well as warm socks – the extremities lose heat faster than the rest of the body.

Other Equipment: It makes sense to have enough money for minor purchases or emergencies. Make sure you have some snack food and enough to drink – water or, in cold weather, a warm drink. A simple first-aid kit is also common sense (plasters, a bandage, nail scissors, painkillers, antiseptic wipes or cream). If you have a mobile phone, take it for emergencies and for the sake of others try to keep it turned OFF unless you really need to use it. A lightweight backpack ("day pack") is the easiest way to carry everything and keep your hands free for stiles, photography, maps – and this guidebook.

Access: The North Cheshire Way is entirely on public roads, public paths or alternative permissive routes agreed with the landowners. The paths shown on the maps in this book are *not* necessarily public rights of way (although the vast majority of them are). It is your right to use public rights of way, but remember that they may cross private land, so keep to the path and respect private property. A small part of the path near its eastern end runs through Lyme Park, which is owned and managed by the National Trust and partly financed by Stockport Metropolitan Borough Council. As the park is closed at night, an alternative route is provided (see Chapter 10) for early risers and night owls!

Countryside Code: PLEASE remember that your enjoyment of the countryside should not detract from the pleasure of other users nor interfere with those who live and work in the country. Good practice is to follow the "Countryside Code"; it is too long to reproduce here, but see the summary below or go to www.countrysideaccess.gov.uk/things_to_know/countryside_code.

Be safe - plan ahead and follow any signs.
Leave gates and property as you find them.
Protect plants and animals, and take your litter home.
Keep dogs under close control.
Consider other people.

Cheshire Dialect
Aimer Gate – a short cut
Mulsh – wet drizzly weather

DISTANCE CHECKLIST

Section	Section		Cumulative	
	km	Miles	km	Miles
1. Hooton to Capenhurst	5.9	3.7	5.9	3.7
Capenhurst to Backford	5.9	3.6	11.8	7.3
2. Backford to the River Gowy	5.8	3.6	17.6	11.0
River Gowy to Dunham-on-the-Hill	5.9	3.7	23.5	14.6
3. Dunham-on-the-Hill to Alvanley	5.3	3.3	28.8	17.9
Alvanley to Frodsham Hill	5.6	3.5	34.4	21.3
4. Frodsham Hill to the River Weaver	5.7	3.6	40.1	24.9
River Weaver to Dutton Locks	5.5	3.4	45.6	28.3
5. Dutton Locks to Barnton	5.9	3.7	51.5	32.0
Barnton to Budworth Mere	6.1	3.8	57.5	35.8
6. Budworth Mere to Arley	5.7	3.6	63.3	39.3
Arley to Tabley	5.9	3.7	69.2	43.0
7. Tabley to Shaw Heath	6.0	3.8	75.2	46.7
Shaw Heath to the River Bollin	5.8	3.6	81.0	50.3
8. River Bollin to Wilmslow	6.2	3.9	87.2	54.2
Wilmslow to Alderley Edge	5.3	3.3	92.5	57.5
9. Alderley Edge to Mottram St. Andrew	5.5	3.4	98.0	60.9
Mottram St. Andrew to the Macclesfield Canal	5.5	3.4	103.5	64.3
10. Macclesfield Canal to Lyme Park	5.6	3.5	109.1	67.8
Lyme Park to Disley	5.0	3.1	114.1	70.9
1a. Chester Spur (Chester to Croughton)	*9.6*	*6.0*		

Note: The section numbers above correspond to the chapter numbers in this guide. Each chapter has two maps and covers two sections. Each section (half-chapter) typically covers 5-6 km (3-4 miles) for which an average walker should estimate 60-90 minutes walking time.

Some are gentle ...

... others are cheeky.

Some just follow the crowd ...

... others like to be boss!

it's best to just
take your time ...
and enjoy the
North Cheshire Way

Characters seen along the North Cheshire Way ...
... whoever you are, there's something for you!

INTRODUCTION

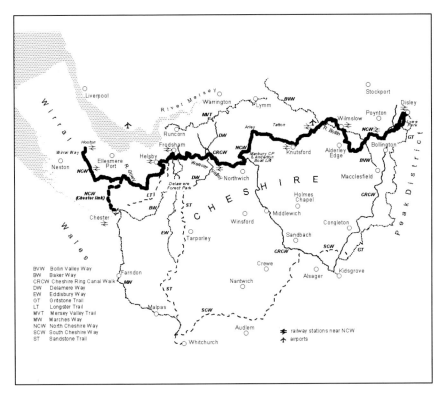

The North Cheshire Way

Cheshire's longest long-distance footpath runs for 114 km (71 miles) from Hooton Station, in Wirral, to Disley Station on the edge of the hills of the Dark Peak. The route crosses the county of Cheshire from west to east through a wide variety of scenery. A 10 km (6 mile) spur route starts at Chester Station and joins the main line of the route beside the Ellesmere Branch of the Shropshire Union Canal at Croughton Bridge. The route links with a number of other medium- and long-distance trails. At Hooton Station the North Cheshire Way (NCW) links with the Wirral Way. At Disley Station it links with the Gritstone Trail and thus the E2 European Long Distance Route. At Chester Station there are links to the Baker Way and the Marches Way. Along its route, there are also links to: the Bollin Valley Way, the Canalside Trail (Chester Canal), the Cheshire Ring Canal Walk, the Delamere Way, the Eddisbury Way, the Ladybrook Valley Interest Trail, the Longster Trail, the Middlewood Way, National Cycleways 5 and 56 and to the Sandstone Trail.

The concept of the North Cheshire Way was developed by The Mid-Cheshire Footpath Society (MCFS) to provide an east-west route across the north of the county to parallel the South Cheshire Way (also created by the MCFS) in the south. Two north-south paths – the Marches Way in the west and the Gritstone Trail in the east join the North and South Cheshire Ways to form the "Cheshire Square". This provides a 250 km perambulation around the entire perimeter of the county that could present a considerable challenge to walkers at the same time as providing a very complete sample of the many delights that Cheshire has to offer.

We hope this book will give you a "slice of Cheshire" … and an incentive to get your boots on and try part of the North Cheshire Way ... or, better still, the whole of it. Welcome to our Cheshire!

Who's coming? – North Cheshire Way at the Cage, Lyme Park

The Landscape along the Route

By "landscape" we mean not only the natural landscape that gives the countryside its shape and texture, but also the way in which man has adapted and changed this natural palette. We think of agriculture and industry, of history and industrial archaeology – and of the huge social changes that have accompanied all of this.

From the industrial towns along the Mersey estuary in the west to the foothills of the Pennines in the east, the North Cheshire Way is full of variety and surprises. Old manor houses, mills and churches give a taste of Cheshire past … and even further back in the mists of time lie the hill forts of the sandstone ridge. The transition to the busy industrial world of today is marked by the Weaver Navigation and the Trent & Mersey Canal, with the unique Anderton Boat Lift. Nature lovers will find much to enjoy with the rich variety of flora and fauna. A constant counterpoint to the changing scene along the route is the farmed landscape so typical of the county: fields of cereals, potatoes and oil-seed rape, cow pasture, market gardens and, in the east, upland sheep farming. Last but not least, there is the wealth of human interest reflected in a wealth of folklore and anecdotes … some comical, some tragic. This is essentially a low-level trail and for much of its length it does not exceed the 100m contour crossing the beautiful and lush countryside of the Cheshire Plain and its associated river valleys, notably the Gowy in the west and the Weaver in its mid-section. There are also hilly sections where the underlying sandstone breaks through the glacial deposits and forms steep ridges that are all the more impressive for being set in the surrounding plain. Around Helsby and Frodsham, the path crosses the sandstone ridge, climbing to around 140m at the viewpoints of Helsby and Frodsham hills. Further east, the sharp escarpment of Alderley Edge, rising to almost 200m, intervenes between two forays into the valley of the River Bollin. And at its eastern end, the North Cheshire Way climbs up into the hills and moors of the Peak District, reaching almost 300m at its highest point near Keeper's Cottage before descending into the Goyt valley at Disley.

The route crosses the grain of the county, taking in as it does some of the finest natural and man-made features of North Cheshire. It touches on three rivers – the Gowy, the Weaver and the Bollin – each draining into the Irish Sea by way of the Mersey and each with its own distinctive character. It climbs over low hills formed by sandstones deposited in near-desert conditions during the Triassic period between 200 and 250 million years ago and reshaped much more recently by the action of ice and water. In the east, the route crosses the border between the softer rocks and glacial deposits of the Cheshire plain and the older and harder gritstones, which form the north-western Peak District.

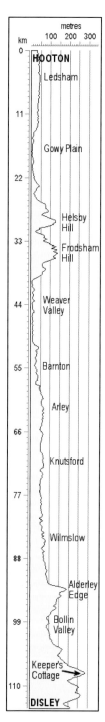

km	metres
	100 200 300
0	
	HOOTON
	Ledsham
11	
	Gowy Plain
22	
	Helsby Hill
33	Frodsham Hill
44	Weaver Valley
55	Barnton
	Arley
66	
	Knutsford
77	
	Wilmslow
88	
	Alderley Edge
99	Bollin Valley
	Keeper's Cottage
110	**DISLEY**

Covering much of this underlying "solid geology" are the extensive deposits left behind by the glaciers and responsible for the richness of much of Cheshire's farmland –

typically the heavy boulder clays of the Cheshire Plain, with lighter sandy soils on the higher ground and silts and sands deposited by the retreating glaciers and rivers in the valleys.

During the Triassic age, much of the area was covered by a large shallow salt lake that evaporated slowly in the tropical sun to leave the deposits of salt that lie deep under much of central northern Cheshire. The topmost level of these salt deposits is slowly dissolved by percolating water, causing the land above to subside and creating shallow depressions that often became filled with water to create many of the Cheshire lakes, known locally as "meres". Other ponds and lakes formed in depressions scooped out by the retreating glaciers. Yet others are the result of human activity – formed by subsidence due to the extraction of the salt beneath. These are locally known as "flashes" – and some did indeed appear "in a flash", almost overnight.

The northern edge of Cheshire borders on the heavily populated conurbations of Merseyside and Greater Manchester, mostly to the north across the River Mersey that formed the natural and historical boundary of Cheshire before the local government changes of recent decades. The heavy industry – chemicals and metalworking, oil refining, heavy engineering and shipbuilding – that characterised this region spilled over into Cheshire, particularly in the eastern Wirral, at Ellesmere Port and Runcorn. Older industries – especially the textile industries – once under-pinned the economic pattern of the north-eastern fringe of the county, making good use of the ample supply of power from the many streams descending westwards from the Pennine hills that form the county's eastern border. In the second half of the 18th century, with the coming of the Industrial Revolution, the textile industry – mostly "King Cotton" west of the Pennines – underwent massive change and explosive expansion. What had been quite literally a cottage industry moved into the towns and, where water power was available, great mills grew up along the Pennine fringe. The people in turn moved from the countryside to the towns where jobs were to be had. The resulting changes were not only economic but also social – and ultimately political – in their consequences. The story is well told at Styal Mill part way along the North Cheshire Way.

Two hundred years later, the major economic changes of the second half of the 20th century have largely replaced these heavier industries with a multi-faceted pattern of more modern light industries – often rooted in advanced technologies and using the skills of the workforce displaced from the shrinking and closing factories of the "old economy". Yet much remains; the interest is nowadays more often in the picturesque aspects of industrial archaeology, telling the story of how our parents and grandparents lived and worked.

Market gardens fringe the northern industrial areas, supplying food to the workers who migrated from the countryside to the burgeoning cities of the industrial revolution, never to return. Further south, and characteristic of much of the central portion of the route, the economy remains – as it has long been – predominantly agricultural. The farming is a mixture of arable and pastoral, but dairy farming dominates on the low-lying and lush grasslands of the Cheshire plain. Not for nothing is Cheshire perhaps best known for its "Cheshire Cheese"; it remains one of the premier dairying regions of Europe. Elsewhere, sheep farming takes over on the higher and drier ground – above all on the hilly land in the Pennine foothills to the east. Interspersed are mixed and arable farms growing cereals (mostly wheat and barley – and increasingly maize) and root crops (potatoes, turnips and swedes). Increasingly, fields of newer crops are appearing, such as rapeseed (for oil and fodder) and linseed.

In such an intensively farmed landscape, there are few remaining signs of the original ecosystems. In prehistoric times, most of Cheshire was covered with broad-leaved forest in which oak predominated, accompanied by elm, lime and hazel, with alder, birch, willow and ash trees on the wetter parts of the lowlands. By Tudor times almost all of these woodlands had been cleared and today only relics remain. These are best seen in the steep-sided valleys ("cloughs") that drain into the main river system, e.g. along the lower Weaver Valley.

The human history of Cheshire began as the ice sheets of the last glaciation retreated northwards about 12,000 years ago. Hunter-fisher folk moved north through the forests but left only minimal traces in the form of artefacts such as flint tools. The first farmers arrived in about 3000 B.C., followed a thousand years later by the first metal users. There remain traces of the Bronze Age in the form of burial mounds ("tumuli"), but more striking are the relics of the Celtic peoples of the Iron Age (from 550 B.C.) – especially the hill forts such as the one at Helsby.

An enormous change to the landscape came with the arrival of the Romans, who dominated (but did not really conquer) the local Celtic tribes (the Cornovii) and established fortresses and garrisons – most notably Deva (now Chester) in 76-77 A.D. – and built a system of roads of which traces still remain. After the departure of the Romans, the confused period of the so-called Dark Ages was followed by the westward migration of the Anglo-Saxon peoples. Cheshire became part of the midland kingdom of Mercia and – like much of northern Britain – also experienced raids and periodic conquest by the Vikings.

Autumn on the North Cheshire Way at Woodhouses

Another enormous change came after the Norman Conquest of 1066 that ended the Anglo-Saxon hegemony of England and brought in a Norman ruling class. At the time of the Domesday Book (1086), Cheshire was at the north-west extremity of the Norman realm and was a rather poor and remote country region – largely wild and wooded apart from the inhabited river valleys. The Normans established the earldom of Chester and large parts of the county were appropriated by the king and the earls for hunting. The North Cheshire Way passes through the area of the great Forest of Mare and Mondrum – of which Delamere Forest, just south of the route, is the largest (but still tiny) relic. With the passing of the centuries, Cheshire became part of Mediaeval England – with the regulation of agriculture by the seasons, of trade by the growing market towns, of the people by the landed nobility and of their souls by the all-pervading Christian church.

Despite its position on the Welsh border, not many castles were built in Cheshire. Its glory became, and largely remains, its wealth of country houses large and small. The county has an exceptional number of these – some dating back to the Middle Ages, others built in the Tudor, Stuart and Georgian periods during the 16th, 17th and 18th centuries. Many of these houses lie on or near the route of the North Cheshire Way – as at Arley Hall, Adlington Hall and Lyme Hall.

The rapid industrialisation of Britain that followed the Industrial Revolution of the late 18th and early 19th centuries made huge changes to the landscape – and yet, paradoxically, left the agricultural heartland relatively undisturbed. Factories developed in Chester, Ellesmere Port, Northwich and – above all – Manchester, Stockport and their surrounding towns and villages. Textile industries predominated in the east and chemicals, metal industries and flour milling in the centre and west.

One industry that had been a key factor in the Cheshire economy since Roman times was the extraction and refining of salt from the gargantuan underground deposits laid down from the Triassic seas and now deep underground through much of north central Cheshire. Vital since olden times for the preservation of foodstuffs, salt – with coal from the Lancashire coalfields to the north and limestone from the White Peak to the east – became the foundation stone of one of the earliest (and soon one of the largest) concentrations of chemical industry in the world. Although this industry is now modernising and downsizing with the development of more efficient and cleaner technology, much remains and the chemical industrial archaeologist will not go wanting, especially around Runcorn and Northwich.

With industrialisation came major changes in transportation. The old turnpike roads were no longer adequate and were replaced and augmented – first by Cheshire's extensive network of canals (now frequented by pleasure craft, but built as vital industrial arteries to take raw materials to, and finished goods from, the factories). The railways soon followed the canals, bringing higher speeds and more efficient goods handling. The second half of the 20th century brought the decline of the railways and the building of a motorway network such that the majority of goods are now carried by the roads that are shared with the private motorist, the horse rider and the long-suffering pedestrian. Politicians call this "progress"; others may not share that view – history will tell!

All this and more lies ahead … but now it's time to don our walking boots and start to walk the *North Cheshire Way* and see for ourselves …

Chemicals on Merseyside

Lyme Park, near Disley

Two faces of Cheshire – "trade" and "gentry"

Chapter 1. Hooton to Capenhurst

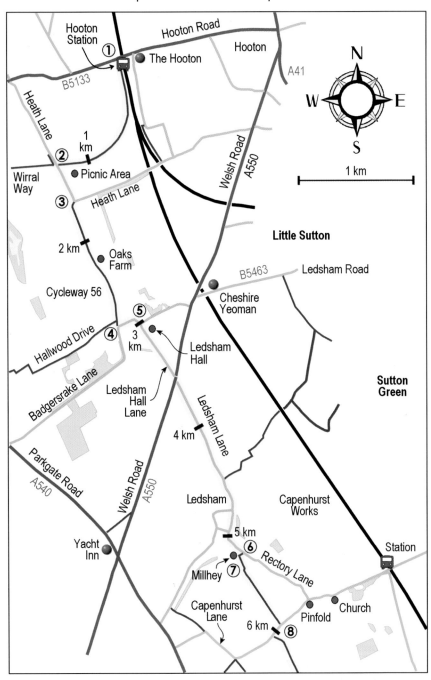

Numbers on the map refer to superscript numbers in the walking instructions

Chapter 1. Hooton to Capenhurst

Hooton – Capenhurst (5.9 km, 3.7 mi):

Leave the station[1] on the Wirral Way. Leave this after 1.3 km at the first bridge[2] (just after a picnic area), climbing up onto Heath Lane. Go left on the lane and where it turns left[3], keep straight ahead on Cycleway no. 56, along a private road past Oaks Farm. On reaching the public road (Badgersrake Lane)[4], go left. Shortly, where the road turns left[5], keep straight ahead on Ledsham Hall Lane, passing Ledsham Hall to reach the A550 (Welsh Road).

Go straight across the main road to continue on Ledsham Lane, passing nurseries and works entrances on your left. About 1½ km after the main road, shortly after the second lane on the right, the lane (now Rectory Lane) bends left with Millhey Farm a little further along on the right. Just after the farm go over a stile[6] on the right and follow the footpath beside a hedge on the right. After the next stile (beside a field gate)[7] continue with the hedge on your left over several stiles, eventually reaching Capenhurst Lane [8].

To continue on the NCW turn right at the lane. Capenhurst village lies some 500m to the left, and the railway station a further 500m in the same direction.

Capenhurst – Hooton (5.9 km, 3.7 mi):

Leave Capenhurst Lane over a stile on the left[8], beside a house with a large stone in the grass near the drive entrance. Go straight ahead on the footpath with the hedge on your right. After just over 500m, where the hedge goes away to your right, go over a stile[7] beside a field gate and continue with the hedge now on your left to reach Rectory Lane[6]. Turn left, going past Millhey Farm, and continue for some 1.6 km to the A550 (Welsh Road).

Go straight across the main road and down Ledsham Hall Lane. Just after passing Ledsham Hall on your right this lane meets another (Badgersrake Lane) at a corner[5]. Go straight ahead, follow the lane around a 45° left-hand bend and in 160m, where the lane turns sharp left[4], take Cycleway no. 56 (signed Willaston Station) on the right. Follow this along a private road past Oaks Farm to reach Heath Lane at a corner[3]. Keep left and continue to follow the cycleway signs until nearing a bridge[2].

Look out for the path on the right (next to a garden and track) giving access to the bed of the former railway that passes under the bridge and is now the Wirral Way. Turn right on the Wirral Way and follow it to Hooton Station[1], the western end of the North Cheshire Way.

Cheshire Dialect
Foxy – wet, marshy
Mizzick – a bog

Cheshire Dialect
Kench – a sprain
Obshackled – limping

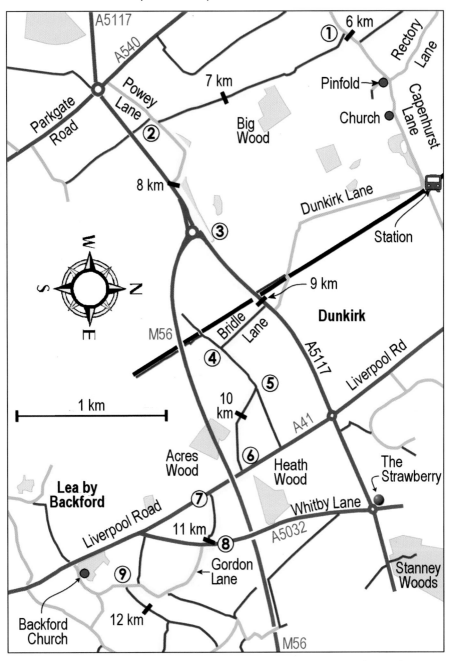

Numbers on the map refer to superscript numbers in the walking instructions

Chapter 1. Capenhurst to Backford

Capenhurst – Backford (5.9 km, 3.6 mi):

Turn right onto Capenhurst Lane and in 120m take a stile[1] on the left into fields. Follow the right-hand hedges to Big Wood, go straight through the wood and exit over a stile into fields. Follow the field boundary on the right, eventually crossing a stile into the corner of a garden. Keep a little to the right and go between hedges to Powey Lane[2].

Go left on the lane to the A5117, then left along the nearside verge. Just after the M56 roundabout[3], cross the A5117 using the central refuge and continue along the right-hand verge. After a railway bridge, go right into Bridle Lane and at the next corner[4] go left on a bridleway. 100m after a gate take a stile[5] on the right. Follow the field edge, over a stile and bridge, between two ponds and over a further stile and bridge into fields.

Go half-left towards the corner of a distant hedge directly under power lines. Cross a stile and follow the power lines to the A41 main road[6]. Cross over, turn right on the far side along the footway and, 180m after going under the M56, go left over a stile[7] through trees and along field edges until nearing a house. Here go right over a stile and left along a hedge to the A5032 main road[8]. Cross over, turn right and in 30m go left on Gordon Lane. Just before the Backford 30-mph zone begins, take a stile[9] on the left into a paddock.

Backford – Capenhurst (5.9 km, 3.6 mi):

Turn right[9] on Gordon Lane and continue to the A5032. Go right and in 30m cross the road to a stile[8] close to the corner of a garden. Follow the hedge; go over a further stile on the right at the end of the garden, then left along the edge of fields and over a stile[7] to the A41.

Go right along the footway, under the M56 and in 80m cross the road to reach a stile[6] into fields. Follow the power lines to a stile at a hedge corner and then go half-right across the open field to a stile in the far corner. Cross the stile, go between two ponds, exit over a stile and bridge into a field and follow the hedge on your left to a stile[5] leading onto a bridleway. Go left on the bridleway and at Bridle Lane[4] turn right for 600m to the A5117.

Go left along the verge and just before the M56 roundabout[3] use the central refuge to cross the A5117. Continue along the verge past the roundabout and take the first road on the right (Powey Lane). Immediately after Ashcroft Cottage[2] take a path between hedges beside the garden, exiting over a stile at the end into fields. Follow field boundaries on your left to Big Wood, go straight ahead through the wood and then along the edge of fields to exit by a stile[1] onto Capenhurst Lane. Go right on the lane and in 100m, beside a house with a large stone in the grass near the drive entrance, cross the road to go over a stile into fields.

Cheshire Dialect
Herb Peter – a cowslip
Paigle – a primrose

Hooton to Backford – the industrial fringe

The first 12 km (7½ miles) of the North Cheshire Way run from Hooton in south Wirral around the edge of the densely populated and quite industrial areas along the south bank of the River Mersey. These built-up areas are themselves linked by tunnel and ferry to the major city of Liverpool across the River Mersey, where it enters the Irish Sea. Although so close to such busy areas, the route itself is mostly rural and the landscape is of medium-sized fields with clipped hedgerows, small copses and field ponds. This farmland landscape of the low-lying parts of the Wirral peninsula derives from the covering of glacial boulder clay that covers the underlying Triassic sandstone. The combination of fertile soils and the proximity of large centres of population has led to a dramatic increase in horticulture in the area, with a high concentration of garden centres and market gardens supplementing more traditional mixed farming.

With the explosive growth of the nearby towns and cities (for example, the population of Ellesmere Port grew from under 4,000 in 1801 to over 80,000 in 2001), the villages have largely lost their rural character and have developed as dormitory settlements for workers in Birkenhead, Liverpool, Ellesmere Port and Chester. Sadly, much of the countryside is disappearing under bricks and mortar. As for the local industry, this too has seen much change. Historically, a stronghold of the "rust belt" heavy industries – shipbuilding, heavy engineering, cars, metals and chemicals – there has been a transition to newer and lighter industry as much of the traditional industrial base succumbs to competition from countries with a lower cost base. Development pressure over the years is also reflected in the dense network of roads, railways and canals in the area.

Hooton and the Wirral Way: The western terminus of the North Cheshire Way is at Hooton Station on the Wirral. From here trains run to Liverpool, Birkenhead, Chester, Warrington, Manchester and beyond. The former Wirral branch line of the Birkenhead Railway joined the main line here. Built in 1886, it closed in 1962 and the track now forms the Wirral Way – a linear country park stretching 19 km (12 miles) from here to West Kirby on the Dee coast. Walkers and cyclists now enjoy the countryside where once steam trains carried day-trippers to the seaside at Parkgate, coal from the colliery at Neston, milk and early potatoes from the Wirral farms. All has changed, the colliery has closed, the farms are becoming housing estates – and the silted Dee has left salt marsh rather than sand at the Parkgate shore.

Standing across the road from Hooton station is the former "Gum Tragasol" works that produced a tragacanth-like gum from the seeds of the carob tree (*Ceratonia siliqua*). The product is still used as a commercial stabiliser and thickener in bakery goods, ice cream, salad dressings and other food products – as well as toothpaste and hair cream.

Chapter 1. Hooton to Backford

The village of Hooton – a mile or so east – was once the seat of the Stanley family, Master Foresters of the Wirral and holders of the "Wirral Horn". Their ownership was held by "cornage" – an ancient tenure of land, which obliged the tenant to give notice of an invasion by blowing a horn.

Hooton had a 15th century timber hall, later replaced by a Georgian manor that was in turn demolished in the 1920s. The site of both now forms part of the huge Vauxhall Motors plant the other side of the M53. The plant also swallowed up much of Hooton Park airfield, which predated Liverpool's John Lennon (Speke) airport across the Mersey. The Hooton Park Trust is attempting to preserve what remains of this First and Second World War fighter base and build a collection of old aircraft and commercial vehicles.

A link with a gentler past is to the Wirral Draghounds, once based here. One Master would entertain his horse in the clubhouse by proffering beer, which his steed would drink from the bottle clenched between its teeth! Probably enough to cause a protest movement these days, if not an Act of Parliament.

Willaston: The village lies a mile or so west of Hooton station and is an old settlement that retains traces of its rural past in its windmill, the (former) farmhouses around the village green and Willaston Old Hall (1558), whose gardens are open at times in the summer. A local curiosity is the "Wirral Stone" – which may have been a milestone, a mounting block or the meeting place of the local court in olden times. A more mundane idea as to a later use of the stone is suggested by an old tithe map that marks it as "The Pissing Stone". Hadlow Road station, on the Wirral Way just south of the village has been preserved in its 1952 condition as a museum.

National Cycleway Route 56 through Ledsham: After leaving the Wirral Way, the NCW follows National Cycleway 56 for most of the way to Capenhurst. This cycle route provides a link for cyclists from Liverpool and Wallasey to Chester. It forms part of the Cheshire Millennium Cycleway and passes through the small village of Ledsham, where Ledsham Hall was the site of a German prisoner of war work camp during World War II.

Capenhurst: From Millhey Farm, footpaths take the NCW into Capenhurst. A reminder of the village's pastoral past is its "pinfold". This is a square sandstone enclosure in which animals were impounded for debts and kept at the owner's expense until redeemed – a custom dating back to Anglo-Saxon times. The village centre lies just east of the route. There is a railway station on the Chester-Liverpool line just 1 km away.

Holy Trinity church, founded in 1859, is shared with Ledsham. The village is perhaps best known locally for distinctively 20th century reasons. The wartime arms factory on the borders of Ledsham and Capenhurst was bought by the Atomic Energy Authority after the Second World War and expanded to become a major nuclear research and production facility. In the past, it produced highly enriched uranium and tritium (radioactive hydrogen) for use in nuclear weapons. The gas diffusion plant (for uranium enrichment) closed in 1982 and is currently being decommissioned, but the Urenco gas centrifuge plant remains in operation, making enriched uranium for civil purposes (nuclear power).

Capenhurst to Backford: The NCW leaves Capenhurst by a footpath leading to Big Wood – an SBI ("Site of Biological Interest") where permissive footpaths lead to the fishing ponds – and onwards across fields and down a lane to the busy A5117 trunk road. There is a short section along the verge of the main road but after passing the Dunkirk Trading Estate, the route finds its way to Bridle Lane and into fields again. The earlier name of this lane, which joined Dunkirk to Saughall before being severed by the building of the M53 motorway, was Coalpit Lane – although coal mining in this area seems unlikely. After crossing the infant Backford Brook, we skirt the private Acres Wood (another SBI), dive under the M53 and enter Backford.

Backford: The village lies on the edge of the Cheshire Plain and on the edge of the Mersey Valley. It stands on a low hill overlooking the "Backford Gap". This is part of the Deva Spillway, the name given to the very low-lying land that links the Dee Valley to the south and west to the Mersey Valley to the north. In fact, it represents the ice-age course of the Mersey when it flowed into the Dee because the Mersey narrows at Liverpool were still blocked by the ice of the Irish Sea. It is an area of mixed farming – in part dairy pasture, with other fields down to grass and maize for silage and some cereal crops.

St. Oswald's church dates from the 13th century and has associations with Birkenhead Priory – the oldest standing building on Merseyside. It has a peal of six bells and seems to have attracted a number of memorable incumbents - including Canon James New, known locally for sharing with his fox terrier the characteristic of having one blue and one brown eye!

Backford Hall is a neo-Tudor house built in the middle of the 19th century on the site of the original 16th century hall. It is now occupied by several departments of Cheshire County Council.

The old hall was the seat of the Birkenhead family and passed to the Glegg family by marriage in 1816. Edward Glegg built the present hall, but when the family's fortunes waned in the 1930s attempts were made to find other uses. It was a country club in the 1930s – until the hasty departure of the proprietor who had a sideline in counterfeit tickets for the Irish lottery. A subsequent attempt to sell it to the Salvatorian Order (a 19th century Roman Catholic foundation) failed, and it passed to the County Council after World War II.

Mr. and Mrs. Maxwell Glegg of Backford Hall

They were the last of the Gleggs to live at Backford – until 1927 – and were known as local characters. Maxwell enjoyed his pint and often had to be rescued from the ditch by his stablemen after failed attempts to drive home from his favoured "watering hole" at Parkgate on the Dee shore. Perhaps his habit in some part reflected an escape from Mrs. Glegg, a formidable lady some twenty stones in weight. When her feud with the owner of nearby Mollington Hall got out of hand in a shop in Chester it took seven stout fellows to restrain her and "remove her to Moston Hospital" whence, sadly, she was never to return to Backford.

Nearby Trails and Places to Visit

Burton and Puddington: 5 km west of Capenhurst - two of the Wirral's prettiest villages.

Chester Zoo: 2 km south of Backford (see Chapter 1a).

Ellesmere Port: 5 km north of Backford, although mostly industrial, the town has the world's largest collection of floating canal craft at its Boat Museum as well as "Blue Planet", the UK's largest aquarium.

Hadlow Road Railway Station: On the Wirral Way at Willaston - restored to its 1952 condition.

Ness Gardens: 7 km west of Capenhurst – Liverpool University's internationally known botanical gardens overlooking the Dee estuary.

Willaston Old Hall: Gardens sometimes open in the summer.

Cheshire Dialect

Bawson – a badger

Jack Nicker – a goldfinch

Chapter 1a. Chester to Blacon

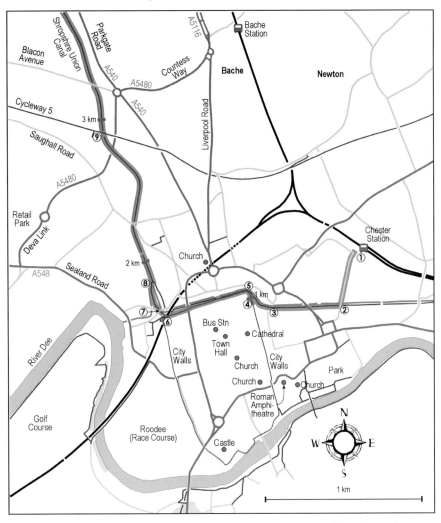

Numbers on the map refer to superscript numbers in the walking instructions

The Ellesmere (Shropshire Union) Canal at Tower Wharf. The canal (1795) runs close by Chester's city walls (Mediaeval on Roman foundations). Telford's Warehouse was built in the 18th century as a canal warehouse and is now a venue for live music and arts events, as well as a popular watering hole.

Chapter 1a. Chester to Blacon

Chester – Blacon (3.0 km, 1.9 mi):

Walk directly away from Chester Station[1] along City Road. In 350m, cross the bridge[2] over the Shropshire Union Canal and descend to the towpath. Follow the towpath, with the canal on your right, for 550m. After the Frog and Nightingale pub[3], go under Frodsham Street bridge, and then in 100m leave the towpath by a winding path that leads to a flight of wooden steps[4] up onto the city walls at Kaleyard Gate. Climb the steps and turn right on the wall, towards the canal. In 40m, at the Phoenix Tower[5], the wall turns 90° to the left and follows the canal below.

Continue on the walls for a further 580m. Immediately after crossing the railway, and just before the 90° left-hand turn of the walls at the Water Tower, leave the walls by a flight of steps[6] on the <u>right</u> and descend to a path that joins a service road and emerges onto the public road at the Y-junction[7] of Tower Road and South View Road. Cross both roads to a white kissing gate that leads onto a canal-side path with the main line of the Shropshire Union Canal on your right and the Dee Branch of the canal at a lower level on your left. In 170m, after passing a boatyard on your left, turn right to cross the main canal at bridge 126[8] and then turn left along the towpath with the canal now on your left. Continue on the towpath for 1 km to reach the bridge[9] at Blacon carrying National Cycleway 5 over the canal.

Note: To avoid the steps to and from the city walls it is also possible simply to continue along the canal towpath for this section.

Blacon – Chester (3.0 km, 1.9 mi):

From the bridge[9] carrying National Cycleway 5 over the Shropshire Union Canal continue south on the towpath with the canal on your right. In 1 km, at bridge 126[8], cross the canal to the boatyard opposite and turn left to follow the canal-side path for 170m (with the main canal now on the left and its Dee Branch at a lower level on the right) to reach South View Road at its Y-junction[7] with Tower Road. Cross both roads and go straight ahead on a small service road and then a path that leads to a flight of steps[6] up onto the city walls. Turn left on the walls, with the Water Tower just behind you, and immediately cross over the railway.

Continue on the walls for 580m and then at the Phoenix Tower[5], follow the walls round a 90° turn to the right. In about 40m, look for wooden steps[4] down on the left. Descend the steps and follow the winding path to the canal towpath ahead. Turn right and follow the towpath, with the canal on your left, for 550m to City Road bridge[2] (number 123B – the fourth bridge). Leave the towpath here and ascend to City Road. Cross the canal and go straight down City Road for 350m to Chester Station[1].

Note: To avoid the steps to and from the city walls it is also possible simply to continue along the canal towpath for this section.

Cheshire Dialect

Blart – to moo (like a cow, from 'bleat')
Shippen – a cowshed (from 'sheep pen')
... well it's different in Cheshire!

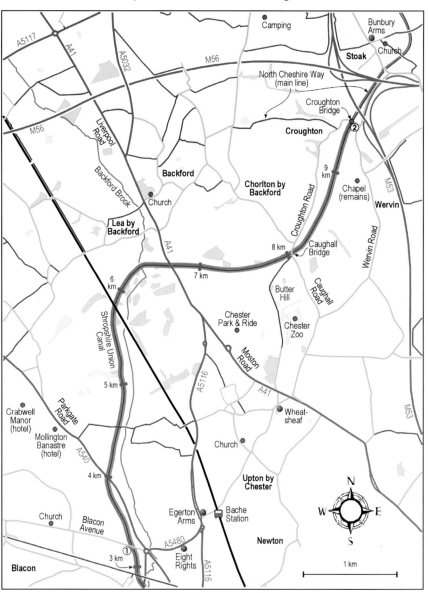

Numbers on the map refer to superscript numbers in the walking instructions

Chapter 1a. Blacon to Croughton

Blacon – Croughton (6.4 km, 4.0 mi):

Pass under the bridge[1] at Blacon that carries National Cycleway 5 over the canal. Continue along the canal towpath with the canal always on your left. In 6.4 km, at Croughton Bridge[2] (no. 135), go under the bridge and join the eastbound main line of the North Cheshire Way (to Disley) that continues north along the towpath and under the M53 motorway ahead.

To join the westbound main line of the North Cheshire Way (to Hooton), turn sharp right from the towpath immediately after passing under Croughton Bridge and ascend the metalled path to the road above. Turn right on the road, crossing the canal and continue on the North Cheshire Way (west). See Chapter 2, key point 9.

Croughton – Blacon (6.4 km, 4.0 mi):

At Croughton Bridge[2] (no. 135), leave the westbound main line of the North Cheshire Way (from Disley) by continuing straight ahead on the towpath, passing under the bridge. Continue on the towpath with the Shropshire Union Canal always on your right. In 6.4 km arrive at the bridge[1] at Blacon that carries National Cycleway 5 over the canal.

If approaching from the eastbound main line of the North Cheshire Way (from Hooton), leave the main line immediately after crossing over the canal at Croughton Bridge, taking the metalled path on the left that descends to the canal towpath. At the towpath, turn left and double back under Croughton Bridge. Continue on the towpath as above. See Chapter 2, key point 9.

Shropshire Union Canal

The canal had its origin in the Chester Canal that ran from Chester and the River Dee to Nantwich and was constructed in 1772. The Ellesmere Canal from Chester to Ellesmere Port on the Mersey (beside which runs the Chester Spur of the North Cheshire Way) followed in 1796, linking Mersey and Dee. Various corporate changes, and the extension of the canal south to the Midlands, resulted in today's Shropshire Union. The link to the Dee remains navigable down three locks beside Tower Wharf on the NCW, while the former Ellesmere Canal accompanies the path from the junction at Tower Wharf to Croughton Bridge, passing through quiet countryside, once a premier region for producing Cheshire cheese.

The canal twice encounters its great competitor, the railway – passing under the 1846 Chester & Holyhead line by the city wall near Bonewaldesthorne's Tower and under the impressive Victorian viaduct of the Birkenhead line (1840) near Lea-by-Backford. Between the two crossings is the Deva Aqueduct carrying the canal over the A5480 at Abbot's Meads.

At Butter Hill, near Chester Zoo, and also near Chorlton-by-Backford, strategic oil storage depots are visible from the canal. These form part of the "secret" Government Pipelines and Storage System (GPSS). High pressure (725 psi) underground oil pipelines connect the Backford site to the nearby Stanlow oil refineries as well as to the Severn estuary, the Humber, the Isle of Grain, the Solent and Aldermaston.

Chester to Croughton – the Chester Spur

Although the main line of the North Cheshire Way runs from Wirral to Disley, the importance of Chester as a tourist destination, county town and focal point for public transport led us to create a "spur". This starts at the railway station in Chester and runs north for 10 km (6 miles) to join the main line at Croughton Bridge on the Shropshire Union Canal. The route follows the canal through the geographical feature known as the Deva Spillway. This is a band of low-lying land that, just like the canal that makes good use of it, links the River Dee to the River Mersey. It represents the former course of the Mersey in the ice age when it could not reach the Irish Sea, as the narrows at Liverpool were still blocked by ice. Instead, it flowed as a tributary into the Dee near Chester. Once the route has left the suburbs of Chester, it crosses a thinly populated area of farmland. The scene is surprisingly rural so close to the towns of Chester and Ellesmere Port and the canal is a wildlife corridor.

Chester: The area was inhabited in the Stone Age. Neolithic pottery has been found near the cathedral and plough marks beneath the former Roman parade ground. Worked flints found near the zoo date back even further to the Mesolithic. But it is as a Roman city that Chester ("Deva" to the Romans) first became a sizeable settlement that was to become one of the three great legionary fortresses of Britannia. The first permanent fort was built around A.D. 70 and stood at the frontier of the Roman Empire, facing the Celtic tribes of the Welsh hills. Its position on the Dee also gave it prominence in providing naval support to Roman campaigns. The Roman town had a piped water supply, public baths, an amphitheatre for public entertainment and buildings with mosaic floors, glazed windows and central heating.

The city declined after the Romans left around A.D. 400, although there is evidence of early Saxon occupation and of Viking raids. It was not until A.D. 907 that King Alfred's daughter Æthelflæd re-fortified the city against Irish-Viking attack and the city grew in importance once more. The cathedral of St. Werburgh and some of the churches are also 10th century in origin and conflict turned to prosperity with the development of the port and a lively trade with the Irish and Scandinavian Norse. The thriving Saxon city did not at first take kindly to the Norman conquerors and, after an uprising in 1069-70, paid the price. There was considerable destruction, a motte and bailey castle was built and the city and county given to Hugh d'Avranches, 1st Earl of Chester. Hugh, known as "Lupus" (the wolf) His successors established a powerful earldom and border conflict with the Welsh continued until the late 13th century, by which time English dominion was established throughout North Wales.

Through the succeeding centuries, Chester continued to prosper as a major religious, administrative, commercial and trading centre. By the early 16th century.

the city was quite cosmopolitan. Wealthy merchants and traders lived alongside the many administrators of this regional centre and the considerable (and wealthy) religious community. Chester had become a major regional centre and the gateway for trade with Ireland. Its mediaeval prosperity, well managed by the powerful guilds, is reflected in the surviving buildings and the unique "Rows" – two-story pedestrian shopping streets that are Chester's iconic equivalent to London's red double-decker bus.

The century following the Tudor heyday of Chester was not easy. There were outbreaks of plague, and religious and political conflict grew early in the 17th century, culminating in the Civil War (1642-6). Chester at first tried to stay neutral, but its strategic importance was too great and the city, under the Royalists, was besieged and fell to the Parliamentarians in 1646. Post-war recovery was slow and Chester never fully regained its mediaeval prosperity or religious importance, although it remained a key administrative centre and increasingly a "county resort". The Dee began to silt and became difficult to navigate, so the port slowly declined as Liverpool and Manchester grew and prospered. Thus the city was relatively unaffected by the rapid growth and industrialisation along the Mersey valley and in the mid-Cheshire salt-fields. Though no longer a port, the arrival of the railways in the mid-19th century brought a "mini-boom". However, the mostly craft-based industries proved uncompetitive and it was as a regional and retail centre – and increasingly as a tourist destination – that Chester flourished as the 19th century ended. Modern Chester is once more a flourishing and prosperous city, with its success now largely supported by the twin pillars of tourism and the retail and service industries.

Nearby Trails and Places to Visit:

Chester: Roman remains (shrine, amphitheatre, temple gardens, hypocaust), almost complete mediaeval city walls and shopping "rows", cathedral and several ancient churches. Shopping, restaurants and bars, accommodation. Chester Zoo is close to the NCW and is bisected by a public bridleway offering the unusual prospect of viewing elephants while walking in Cheshire. The Shropshire Union Canal runs below the city walls with a flight of locks just east of Tower Wharf (see boxes on pages 24 and 27).

Trails: Several long-distance trails converge on the NCW in Chester. The *Baker Way* runs from the station eastwards for 22 km to Delamere Forest. The *Marches Way* runs from the station southwards along the Welsh border, intersecting with the South Cheshire Way near Whitchurch to form, with the Gritstone Trail, the "Cheshire Square" (see page 10). The *Longster Trail* does not reach the NCW here but is accessible by local bus and runs for 15 km from the edge of Chester to meet the NCW again at Helsby Hill. The *Mercian Way*, part of National Cycleway 45, runs south from Chester to Bewdley.

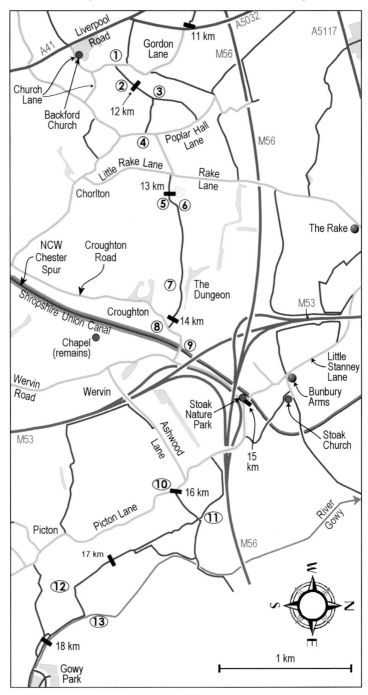

Numbers on the map refer to superscript numbers in the walking instructions

Chapter 2. Backford to the River Gowy

Backford – River Gowy (5.8 km, 3.6 mi):

Just before the 30 mph limit, go left over a stile[1] and cross a paddock diagonally to the far left corner. Cross a wooden 2-rail fence, go down a grass track between paddocks and over a stile[2] into a large field. Go straight ahead to a stile[3] in the far hedge, then immediately right along the field edge. In the next field, where the hedge veers right, keep straight ahead to reach a lane[4].

Go left on the lane and at a T-junction go straight across the road and over a stile opposite. Follow the hedge to a "sentry box"[5]; go left and shortly, at a second "sentry box"[6], go right along the field edge to the edge of woodland. Go right over a footbridge[7] and then left along the field edge with a wooded valley on your left. At the end of the field, go over a stile and keep left alongside a coach depot. Go left at the lane[8] and continue to a canal bridge (no. 135). Descend left onto the towpath; the Chester Spur joins here[9] ... see Chapter 1a. Go under the M53 and M56 and at the next bridge (no. 136) leave the towpath, crossing the old canal bridge and going up onto Picton Lane.

Go sharp right on the lane, crossing back over the canal and then over the M56. After a lane leaves on the right, take the next path on the left[10] down a green lane. Where this ends, at a crossing of paths[11], go right along the field edge with a drainage dyke on your left. Continue beside the dyke for 1.1 km and then go left over a footbridge[12]. Go along the edge of two fields with another dyke on your left and then over another footbridge to reach the embankment[13] of the River Gowy. Turn right and follow the embankment.

River Gowy – Backford (5.8 km, 3.6 mi):

Leave the River Gowy where the footpath turns left[13] over a footbridge. Go along the edge of two fields and at the end of the second field cross over a footbridge[12] and immediately turn right and follow the path for 1.1 km beside a drainage dyke on your right. On reaching a crossing of paths[11], turn left along a green lane to reach a lane[10]. Turn right, go over the M56 and keep straight ahead.

Just after crossing the road bridge over the canal, go sharp left down a track back over the old canal bridge and onto the towpath. Follow the towpath under the M56 and M53 to the next bridge (no. 135); the Chester Spur joins here[9] ... see Chapter 1a. Climb up onto the road and turn right, back over the canal bridge. At a finger post[8] in 200m, go over a stile and follow the path beside a coach depot and then into fields. Go along the edge of two fields, turn right over a footbridge[7] and immediately left along the edge of two fields to a "sentry box"[6]. Turn left here and shortly, at a second "sentry box"[5], turn right and follow the hedge to emerge on Little Rake Lane.

Go straight across the road and down Rake Lane opposite. 80m after a left-hand bend go over a stile[4] on the right. Keep straight ahead and in the second field go over a stile[3] through the hedge on the left. Keep straight ahead across a large field to cross a stile[2] in the far hedge onto a grassy track between paddocks. At the end of the track keep ahead over a wooden 2-rail fence into a paddock. Cross diagonally to a stile in the far left corner and turn right[1] on Gordon Lane.

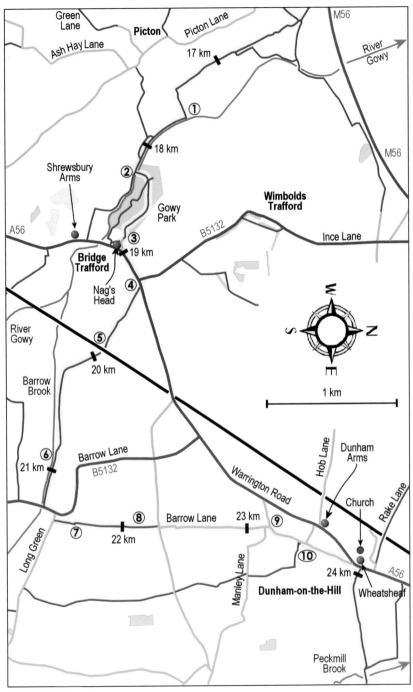

Numbers on the map refer to superscript numbers in the walking instructions

Chapter 2. River Gowy to Dunham-on-the-Hill

River Gowy – Dunham-on-the-Hill (5.9 km, 3.7 mi):

Turn right[1] onto the embankment and follow it with the river on your left as far as a footbridge[2] (not a tractor bridge) on the left. Cross over into Gowy Park and go straight ahead into trees. Follow a clear path through woodland, ignoring side paths, and then across a grassy open space to a kissing gate[3] at the park entrance. Go down the lane to the A56, turn left and just after crossing the B5132 (Ince Lane), cross the main road and go over a stile[4] into fields. Follow the field edge and cross a plank bridge. Cross the field to another bridge and then aim for the railway culvert[5] ahead. After the railway, go straight ahead to a pair of stiles across a farm track and then to a footbridge. Follow the hedge on your left, going round a left-hand corner, and then over stiles either side of a farm drive. Aim slightly right to converge with Barrow Brook near nurseries[6] on the far side and follow it to the B5132 (Barrow Lane).

Go left on the road, and in 110m take Long Green on the right. In 50m go down a farm drive on the left and, at the end, through a gate into fields. Bear slightly left away from the hedge to a footbridge in the far hedge; cross over and shortly after cross a stile in the fence[7] on the left. Continue with the fence on your right to a pair of stiles over a farm track, go over these and very slightly left in the next large field aiming for a footbridge[8]. Go straight ahead after the bridge to reach a lane. Turn right on the lane and immediately left to climb Barrow Lane. At a grassy triangle[9] go ahead and slightly right to enter the village of Dunham-on-the-Hill. The village green[10] is at the top of the hill.

Dunham-on-the-Hill – River Gowy (5.9 km, 3.7 mi):

Continue through the village from the green[10]. In 130m bear left at a grassy triangle[9] and then in 40m keep straight ahead (signed for Barrow) for 800m to a T-junction. Go right and immediately left over a stile, then straight across a field, over a footbridge[8] and bear slightly right across a large field to a pair of stiles at a farm track. Cross over, follow the fence on the left and in 170m cross at a stile[7], continuing with it on your right to a footbridge. Cross over, and bear left to a gate in the field corner and then down the drive onto a lane. Turn right and in 50m left at a T-junction.

Just before a bridge, go right over a stile and follow a brook on your left. After passing nurseries[6] that lie on the other side of the brook, bear slightly right to a pair of stiles either side of a farm drive. Cross the drive and follow the hedge on your right, soon turning right to keep by the hedge and arrive at a footbridge. Cross over and aim for a pair of stiles either side of a farm track and then aim for a culvert[5] under the railway. Go under the railway, across a field to a footbridge, across another field to another footbridge and then beside a hedge to a stile[4] onto the A56. Cross the road and turn left. After crossing the B5132 turn right down Hassall's Lane. At the end go through a kissing gate[3] into Gowy Park. Follow the path across a grassy space and into the main woodland, ignoring all side paths, to reach a footbridge[2] over the River Gowy. Cross over, turn right along the embankment and continue until the path turns left over a footbridge[1].

Backford to Dunham-on-the-Hill – the Gowy Plain

From Backford to Dunham-on-the-Hill the NCW crosses the flat and low-lying flood plain of the River Gowy. Until the final climb into Dunham the entire route lies less than 20m (65 ft) above sea level and even Dunham-on-the-Hill, despite its imposing name, can only aspire to summit at the dizzying height of 42m. At the beginning and end of this part of the route we make our first acquaintance with the Cheshire Plain. This is in fact just part of a larger gently rolling plain – interrupted by sandstone ridges – that extends south from the Mersey Valley beyond Cheshire into western Staffordshire (as far as Stoke-on-Trent and Stafford) and northern Shropshire (as far south as Shrewsbury and Telford). This is a rural landscape and is dominated by dairy farming, merging into more mixed and arable farming in the north. It is a countryside of managed – and at times too intensive – farming, characterised by strong field patterns (an aid to navigating the route!) with many hedgerows, isolated copses – and a quarter of all the field ponds in England and Wales. Villages tend to be small and interspersed by individual large farmsteads – although nearer to the urban areas such as Merseyside, Greater Manchester and Chester this is increasingly modified by the spread of dormitory housing for commuters. Large estates, with associated parkland and woodland, are also characteristic – and many remain in good condition, either in private ownership or held by the National Trust.

The origins of this landscape lie primarily in the effects of glaciation. Although Triassic sandstones and marls underlie the plain, these are thickly covered – except for the central ridge and several smaller outcrops (like Dunham) – by the boulder clay left behind by the retreating glaciers at the end of the last ice age. A clue to what lies beneath is found in the predominant building materials – orange-red brick from the sandy boulder clay and sandstone in walls and in the older cottages and churches.

Historically, this was an area so densely wooded that human settlement came late and at first only on the higher land. The Mersey Valley to the north marked a natural barrier and represented the boundary zone between the Anglo-Saxon kingdom of Mercia to the south and the lands held by the Danes to the north. Even today a Lancastrian will regard his Cheshire neighbour as a "southerner"!

The middle part of the route from Backford to Dunham crosses the lowest land of all – the flood plain of the River Gowy that forms a southward incursion of the Mersey Valley into the Cheshire Plain. The Gowy is a small river, rising near the Peckforton Hills (down the Sandstone Trail to the south), that meanders slowly northward to meet the Mersey at Stanlow Point near Ellesmere Port. Its flood plain is disproportionately wide and until recently was too wet and marshy to be farmed other than as water meadows. Despite some "improvement" and a huge open landfill site at Wimbolds Trafford, much of its character has been preserved and is well seen from the NCW as it follows the Gowy upstream from Stoak to Bridge Trafford.

Backford to Croughton: From Backford the NCW takes a rural route across farmland, although the hum of the busy M56 can be heard to the north with, as the walker approaches Croughton (pronounced *Craw-tun* and not to be confused with Crowton further east), a counterpoint from the M53 ahead. Yet the drivers rushing along the motorways could little imagine the different world that lies just a few hundred metres away – where cows, horses and sheep replace the juggernauts and fishermen dream away an afternoon at The Groves fishery. At Croughton, we reach the Shropshire Union Canal (originally the Ellesmere Canal) and the junction with the Chester Spur of the NCW that starts at Chester Station and joins the main route at the canal bridge *(see Chapter 1a for information on the canal and the Chester Spur)*. The eastbound main route uses the canal towpath to go north and under the two motorways to Stoak.

Stoak: This is an old village beside the canal and, less fortunately, in the shadow of a huge motorway intersection. The description of it by a Victorian historian as "a collection of ragged and filthy hovels" is grossly unfair. The red sandstone parish church is mostly Victorian and the Bunbury Arms dates back to the 16th century.

Gowy meadows: From Stoak to Bridge Trafford we cross the Gowy meadows – an open, perhaps lonely and sometimes windswept, landscape of peaty water meadows criss-crossed by drainage ditches. Its proximity to the 21st century is marked by the "earthworks" of the huge landfill site on the far side of the river and the silhouettes of the oil refineries just 3 km to the north beside the Mersey. With patience, there are waterfowl and marsh birds to be seen, dragonflies and damselflies skim past, lapwings cry and skylarks sing overhead; the ditches have water violets and bladderwort in summer. After crossing the river the NCW passes through the newly created Gowy Park.

Bridge Trafford to Little Barrow: A small settlement straddling the A56 main road from Chester to Helsby at the bridge over the Gowy. The Nag's Head pub lies just off the NCW and in the field between the two can be seen the Oak Fold herd of Highland cattle established in 1995. Crossing the former turnpike road, the NCW continues across open farmland, diving through a culvert under the Chester to Helsby railway line – the former Birkenhead, Lancashire & Cheshire Junction railway, opened in 1850 – before converging with Barrow Brook and reaching the B-road at Little Barrow. The Foxcote, 700m south past the former station is now a seafood pub with a name reflecting railway history in that "Foxcote Manor" was the name of the local train.

Little Barrow to Dunham-on-the-Hill: The final part of this section of the NCW turns back northwards, at first across low-lying farmland and then ascending to the small sandstone outcrop crowned by the village of Dunham-on-the-Hill. Lying just off the main road, this is a pretty village. Many of the houses, several dating back to the 16th and 17th centuries, are built from the local reddish sandstone; some still have wattle-and-daub interior walls and sandstone cellars. The village lanes, too, are in places cut through the raw rock.

A quiet place today, but there is a link to that turbulent period of English history, the Wars of the Roses. Sir John Troutbeck, Lord of Dunham-on-the-Hill, lived not far away at Brimstage Hall on the Wirral. He fell, with many other Lancastrians – "the flower of Cheshire" – at the battle of Blore Heath in 1459 where the Yorkists under Richard Neville, Earl of Salisbury, won the victory that was to lead eventually to the crown passing to the House of York with the accession of Edward IV in 1461.

Nearby Trails and Places to Visit

Gowy Meadows: (Cheshire Wildlife Trust – open to all). Access by the public footpath running west from Thornton-le-Moors church (between the M56 and the A5117). Lowland grazing marsh with intersecting ditches. Flowers, birds and invertebrates.

Manley Mere Adventure Trail: Signposted from the A56. Wind-surfing, adventure trail and refreshments.

Mouldsworth Motor Museum: (Sundays and Bank Holidays). Smithy Lane, Mouldsworth (signed from the A56 via the B5132). Vintage cars and more.

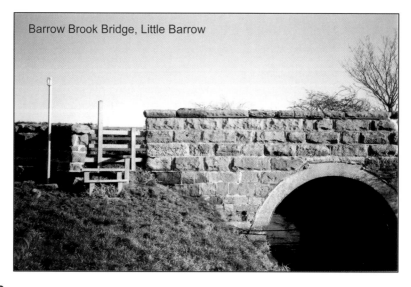

Barrow Brook Bridge, Little Barrow

Wildlife of the Gowy Meadows

Water Violet
(Hottonia palustris)

Lapwing
*(Vanellus
vanellus)*

Water vole
*(Arvicola
terrestris)*

Banded Demoiselle
(Calopteryx splendens)

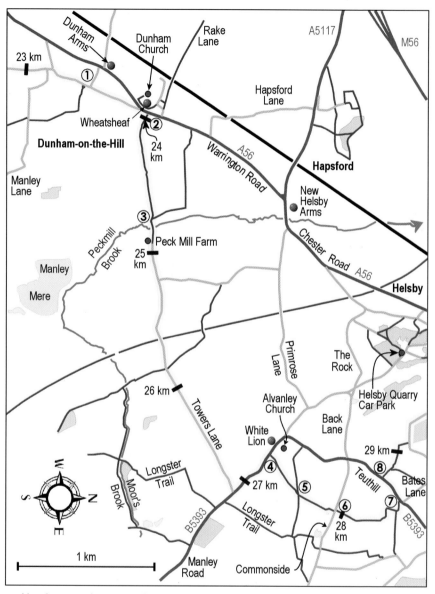

Numbers on the map refer to superscript numbers in the walking instructions

Chapter 3. Dunham-on-the-Hill to Alvanley

Dunham-on-the-Hill – Alvanley (Teuthill) (5.3 km, 3.3 mi):

From the village green[1], continue through the village down to the A56 and turn right. In 50m, go right over a stile[2] and down a green lane. Cross a stile into fields and keep straight ahead over several stiles, with the field boundary on the right. After about ¾km turn right through a metal gate[3] and immediately left to follow the hedge. Cross a concrete bridge and go through a bridleway gate into the yard of Peck Mill Farm. Keep left through the yard and leave by a wooden gate onto a lane. Go straight up this lane for almost 2 km to its T-junction with the B5393 (Manley Road). Turn left and in 400m, just before the White Lion pub, go through a gate[4] on the right into fields.

Keep the fence on your right to the end of the field, and then go right through a kissing gate[5]. Immediately go left through two fields with the hedge now on your left. Go through a kissing gate into a paddock, pass a small pond and walk beside the fence on your right and through a gate onto Commonside Road. Go left and immediately right through a metal gate[6]. Walk downhill with the hedge on your left through two fields, go through a gate and follow the irregular hedge line on your left to the field corner. Go round the corner to the right and downhill with the hedge still on your left to a plank bridge. Go over the bridge and through a kissing gate and turn left along the hedge to reach a kissing gate[7] onto the B5393 (Teuthill). Turn left on the lane and after 320m turn right[8] into a green lane.

Alvanley (Teuthill) – Dunham-on-the-Hill (5.3 km, 3.3 mi):

Turn left[8] onto the B5393 (Teuthill) and in 320m go right through a kissing gate[7] (signed Burrows Lane). In 80m go through a kissing gate on the right, over a plank bridge and straight ahead uphill beside the hedge. At the field corner keep the hedge on your right for another 150m to reach a gate in the hedge on your right. Go through and walk uphill with the hedge on your right to reach a gate onto Commonside[6]. Go left and immediately right between sandstone pillars and through a gate into a paddock. Follow the fence on your left, pass a small pond and then go through a kissing gate into fields. Follow the hedge on your right through two fields and on reaching a field gate do *not* go through but take a narrow gap between hedge and fence to reach a metal kissing gate[5]. Go through and immediately turn left along the hedge and through a gate[4] onto the B5393 (Manley Road).

Turn left and on reaching the derestriction road sign turn right into Towers Lane. Go straight ahead down the lane for almost 2 km to reach Peck Mill Farm. Go through a small wooden gate into the yard, follow the fence on your right and leave the yard by a bridleway gate. Continue in the field with the hedge on your right, cross a concrete bridge and halfway along the edge of the next field go right through a metal gate[3] and immediately left. Follow the field boundaries on your left across several stiles, down a short green lane and over a stile[2] onto the A56 main road. Turn left and in 50m bear left up the lane into Dunham-on-the-Hill. Go straight ahead through the village to the village green[1].

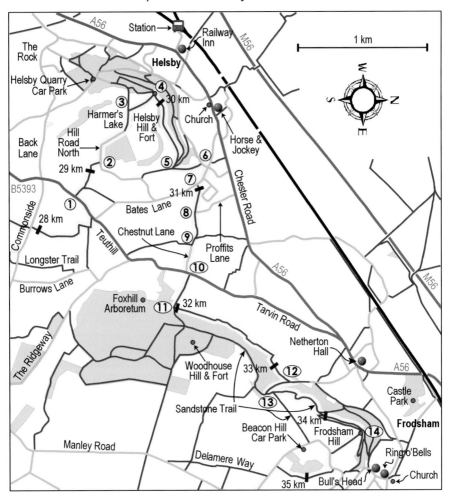

Numbers on the map refer to superscript numbers in the walking instructions

Be safe - plan ahead and follow any signs.
Leave gates and property as you find them.
Protect plants and animals, and take your litter home.
Keep dogs under close control.
Consider other people.

Chapter 3. Alvanley to Frodsham

Alvanley (Teuthill) – Frodsham Hill (5.6 km, 3.5 mi):

Turn right from the road[1] along a green lane. At the end go half-right, diagonally across the field, through a gate and then through a further gate on the right and down a narrow path to the road[2]. Go left on the road until it ends and then keep ahead past Harmer's Lake on the right. At a finger post[3] bear right into National Trust land and take a clear path to the trig. point[4] at the top of Helsby Hill. Leave the summit by going right to a fence corner and take the path downhill through woodland. Keep right and slightly uphill where it forks, descend to a stile at the edge of the woods and then at the finger post[5] go left down to the road[6].

Go right at the crossroads, right again into Bates Lane and in 150m (after the entry to *Landscape Dene*) go left at a finger post[7] down a narrow path between hedges. Go through a gate, across a field corner to Proffits Lane[8], then straight across and follow a clear path to a gate onto a wide track. Cross a footbridge beside a ford[9] and go up the lane to the B5393[10]. Go left, in 30m right up a long drive (signed *The Holt*), then through a gate[11] into woods. Go immediately left along the edge of the woods for 750m. After a grassy area go ahead and then up steps[12] beside a wall. At the top turn right, passing cliffs on your left, to a finger post at the Sandstone Trail. Turn left on this and follow it through the woods. After a flight of steps[13], the Sandstone Trail forks. Do *not* go right onto the golf course, but keep straight ahead on a broad path (Sandstone Trail) through the woods, and *below* the top of the escarpment, to reach the war memorial[14] at the top of Frodsham Hill.

Frodsham Hill – Alvanley (Teuthill) (5.6 km, 3.5 mi):

Turn left at the war memorial[14] onto the Sandstone Trail through woods. Do not leave the woods, but continue and after descending a flight of steps[13] turn right and at the finger posts again right to leave the Sandstone Trail. Descend with cliffs on your right, to the corner of a wall on your left. Go up two steps and descend steps[12] beside the wall. Cross over a grassy area and into the woods. Follow the edge of the woods for 750m, leaving them by a gate[11] on the right and go down a private drive to the B5393 (Tarvin Road). Turn left and in 30m go right[10] down Chestnut Lane to a footbridge beside a ford[9]. Cross and go slightly left through a gate. Cross a field to Proffits Lane[8], then ahead through a gate (signed Helsby), across a field corner and up a narrow path to Bates Lane[7].

Turn right, then left at the crossroads and in 60m go left[6] up a narrow path into woodland. At the top, at a finger post[5], go right over a stile into National Trust land and follow the leftmost path (signed Hill Top) through woods to reach the trig. point[4] at the top of Helsby Hill. Turn directly away from the cliff, go down a broad track that soon narrows between hedge and fence and at a finger post[3] go left (Longster Trail) to pass Harmer's Lake on the left and reach a metalled road. In 340m go right at a finger post (signed Tarvin Road)[2] on a narrow path, through a gate, then immediately left along the field edge and through a gate. Continue diagonally across the next field to a stile in the bottom corner. Go over and down a green lane to the B5393 (Teuthill)[1].

Dunham-on-the-Hill to Frodsham – the Sandstone Ridge

For much of the 11 km from Dunham-on-the-Hill to Frodsham the North Cheshire Way traverses the Cheshire Sandstone Ridge. This provides a total change in the landscape along the route as it climbs from the Gowy plain up to Alvanley and then follows the northern edge of the ridge through Helsby to Frodsham. The ridge is of reddish-pink sandstone and runs for 40 km north-south across the centre of the western part of the county. Although discontinuous and not really very high (still only 141 metres at Helsby Hill) it is very prominent as it rises sharply from the surrounding plain. The lush green fields of the plain are replaced by poorer permanent pastures, with some arable farming on the gentler slopes and mature deciduous and mixed woodland on the steeper scarps facing west and north. On the ridge itself and on its gentler eastern slopes, the combination of the thin sandy soils and the tracts of woodland gives the impression of heathland. The north-facing escarpment at the northern end of the ridge overlooks the marshland of the Mersey Valley and remains a prominent and craggy feature thanks to its resistance to the passage of the Irish Sea ice-sheet, which covered much of Cheshire some 20,000 years ago.

The northern part of the ridge tends to be more sparsely populated, with scattered farms and small villages. This contrasts with the Mersey Valley lying immediately below the northern scarps where large villages – Helsby and Frodsham – stand at the foot of the slope along what became the inner Mersey estuary. In early mediaeval times, Frodsham was a riverside port – the name "Ship Street" survives – but, as the river retreated, the villages became separated from the river by flat and empty marshland. The marshes were still flooded each high tide until the building in the 1880s of the Manchester Ship Canal alongside the river. The marshes remain and sheep still graze in the shadow of the large chemical plants along the Mersey. The NCW itself stays mostly on the higher land and offers views of the marshes, the tidal Mersey and beyond to Runcorn, Liverpool and Merseyside.

Dunham-on-the-Hill to Alvanley: The NCW descends from the village green at Dunham, passing the village school and – opposite – Elder Tree Cottage dating back to 1589 and formerly a coaching inn on the road to Chester. Leaving the village, the route strikes out over the last of the Cheshire Plain, crossing fields – often used for grazing the ponies of the travelling community – to Peck Mill Farm. After the farm, the NCW begins a long slow climb up a quiet lane from the plain to the village of Alvanley at the top of the western escarpment of the Cheshire Sandstone Ridge. On the way, the route crosses a bridge over the dismantled West Cheshire Railway. This opened in 1869 and ran from Mouldsworth to Helsby along the foot of the escarpment but passenger services were short-lived with a regular passenger service only from 1870 to 1875. For most of its life it served as a "mineral line" servicing the former BICC cable works in Helsby. The track has been removed and it is hoped to develop the track bed as a cycle route.

Alvanley: Having reached the top of the hill, the NCW passes close by the mid-Victorian village church of St. John and the local hostelry (the White Lion). Just opposite the church, the village school is the site of Alvanley Community Orchard, which includes a collection of

> ### William Arden, 2nd Baron Alvanley
>
> The Ardernes or Ardens were the local landowners for centuries. The 2nd baron was a notable Regency wit. Emerging unscathed from a duel, he handed a guinea to the hackney driver who had conveyed him to the spot and returned him home. Surprised by such generosity, the driver demurred. "My lord," he marvelled, "I only took you a mile." "The guinea's not for taking me, my man," Alvanley replied. "It's for bringing me back!"

Cheshire varieties of apples and damsons. We then leave the village across fields to the hamlet of Commonside before descending quite steeply into the valley separating the crags at Helsby from those at Frodsham before climbing again to leave the parish at the hamlet of Teuthill.

Helsby: From Teuthill the path climbs steadily for a kilometre to the trigonometric survey point on top of Helsby Hill, passing Harmer's Lake on the way. At 141 metres (462 feet), this is one of the highest points of the Cheshire Sandstone ridge and the spot commands views from the Welsh hills in the west, across the Mersey to the twin cathedrals of Liverpool to the north, south down the ridge to Beeston Castle and eastwards to the Pennine hills. At least in theory the entire 114 km length of the North Cheshire Way is visible from here!

Left:

Helsby from the air.

Right:

Helsby crag.

The hilltop is the site of an Iron Age promontory fort constructed around 800 B.C. by the Cornovii at the northern limits of their tribal lands. The site is protected by the sheer crags on the north and by a clearly visible double arc of ramparts and a ditch to the south. In the skies above may be seen raven, buzzards and – with luck – even peregrine falcons.

As the aerial photograph clearly shows, the village of Helsby lies on the edge of the marshes and hugs the foot of the wooded crag. Sandstone quarrying was an important industry in the 19th century and until the 1920s. Mountskill Quarry had its own tramway link to take the rock to Ince Pier and thence by barge to Liverpool. The disused quarry can be visited and the car park is handy for the NCW on the western slopes of Helsby Hill. Yesterday's industry changed to a pretty spot colonised by rowan, silver birch and willow – a refuge for bats and birds (including woodpeckers), dragonflies and hedgehogs.

Helsby to Frodsham: Leaving Helsby Hill the NCW runs through the woodland near the top of the escarpment before descending sharply to the edge of Helsby village. A short section across fields takes us out of Helsby and into the hamlet of Woodhouses, an outlying part of Frodsham lying at the bottom of the valley that separates the crags of the two villages. We are briefly back in farmland more reminiscent of the Cheshire Plain with cattle, potatoes and cereals. After crossing the ford at Woodhouses, the route climbs a little and then runs for just over a kilometre along the edge of the woods cloaking the northern escarpment of Woodhouse Hill and then Frodsham Hill. The woodland is glorious with bluebells in May and a home for a rich variety of birdlife, including woodpeckers and long-tailed tits. Another Iron Age fort lies high above at the top of the escarpment and can be visited by climbing a very steep path that links to the Sandstone Trail from key point 11 *(see map at the beginning of this chapter)*.

Just after crossing the steep-sided Dunsdale valley, we climb steeply up to join the Sandstone Trail near "Jacob's Ladder" and "Baker's Dozen". The first is a scramble up a rocky crag with footholds for the fit and adventurous, while "Baker's Dozen" refers to the 13 steps that form an alternative for the rest of us. The name remembers Jack Baker, pioneer of many Cheshire walks and a founder of The Mid-Cheshire Footpath Society – the authors of this guide. From the top, the NCW shares its route with the Sandstone Trail, passing through the scarp woodlands and beside more sandstone outcrops to emerge at the War Memorial on the summit of Frodsham Hill (110 metres, 360 feet, and also known as

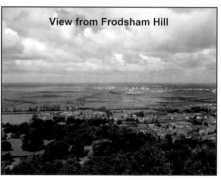

View from Frodsham Hill

Overton Hill). The memorial was built in 1921 from Runcorn sandstone, and was the site of beacons lit for the Silver Jubilee of King George V in 1935, the Festival of Britain 1951 and the Millennium in 2000. There are good views from here across the Mersey Estuary and towards Helsby Hill. The wooden helter-skelter built here in 1908, once a popular outing for the children, was a local landmark until its demolition in 1977.

Frodsham: The little market town was once a fishing port on the Mersey, when it still reached to the foot of the sandstone ridge. It received its charter around 1230 and is regarded as the best surviving example of a planned mediaeval town in Cheshire. The church of St. Laurence stands on the site of a Saxon chapel at the foot of the crag but still high above the town and dates back to Norman times. At Castle Park there was once a castle, but this was destroyed by fire in 1654. The main street – one of the widest in Cheshire – is rich in old buildings and is still the site of a big weekly market.

> **Prince Warabo of Opobo**
>
> King Jaja of Opobo was born in 1821 and sold as a slave at the age of 12. But through his own enterprise in the palm oil trade became one of the most powerful men in the Niger delta and founded the kingdom of Opobo – with himself as king! Soon he became so wealthy that he was able to ship the palm oil himself directly to Liverpool. This contact led in the 1880s to him sending his son, Prince Warabo, to attend the Manor House School (now the Yuet Ben Chinese restaurant) in Frodsham. Sadly, the boy died of pneumonia; his grave remains in the churchyard at Overton.

Nearby Trails and Places to Visit

Castle Park (Frodsham): Art galleries in the Victorian stables, craft workshops and gardens.

Delamere Forest Park: Cheshire's largest area of woodland and part of the former Royal Forest (i.e. hunting grounds) of Mare and Mondrum. Accessible via the Sandstone Trail. Walks and cycle trails, visitor centre, wildlife.

Foxhill Arboretum: Tarvin Road, Frodsham; open to the public most weekends. The former home of Dr. Lawrence Pilkington (of the glass-making family). He bequeathed house and grounds to the Diocese of Chester, which uses the estate as a conference centre. Azaleas and rhododendrons, dove tree, eucalyptus, special collections of conifers and of Chilean plants.

Helsby Quarry Woodland Park: Nature reserve owned and managed by Vale Royal Borough Council. Convenient car parking for the NCW at Helsby Hill.

Longster Trail: Runs close to the NCW through Alvanley and meets it at the top of Helsby Hill. It is a waymarked route created and maintained by The Mid-Cheshire Footpath Society and runs for 15 km (10 miles) from Helsby to Piper's Ash on the outskirts of Chester.

Sandstone Trail: Runs with the NCW for a short way south of Frodsham Hill. This trail starts in Frodsham and runs for 51 km (32 miles) south along the Cheshire Sandstone Ridge to Whitchurch, just over the border in Shropshire.

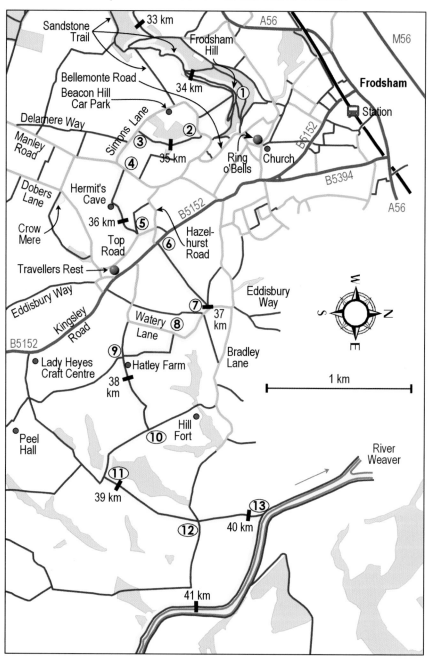

Numbers on the map refer to superscript numbers in the walking instructions

Chapter 4. Frodsham to the River Weaver

Frodsham Hill – River Weaver (5.7 km, 3.6 mi):

Walk away from the war memorial[1] to iron gates onto the road. Go left, and take the first path right[2] around the hillside; pass a hotel on the right, and go down to Simons Lane[3]. Go left, left again at a T-junction and in 70m go right through a gate[4]. Follow the left-hand hedge, soon turning left with caves on the right. Go through a gate on the left and <u>diagonally</u> across the next field, keeping uphill of a hollow, to a gate in the far corner[5,] then left along a road. Go right at a T-junction and down to the B5152. Go left then at once right through a squeeze stile[6] and along the right-hand hedge over stiles to a lane[7]. Go right and, 90m after a right-hand bend, up the left bank, over a stile[8] and beside a hedge on your right. In 130m, cross a stile in the hedge and go diagonally across the next field, aiming to the left of the tall trees, to cross a stile. Go right and cross to a stile next to a field gate and onto a farm road[9].

Go left on the road to the farm and leave the yard by a stile in the far right corner. Follow the hedge and cross a stile. Follow the fence on the right to cross a stile[10] on the right. Cross to the far left corner of the field and wood. Just after a pond surrounded by trees, enter woods by a stile on the left. Descend to a stream, then zigzag up and exit the wood by a stile. Go ahead to a waymark post[11] before houses, then left towards a stile and cross the next field to a kissing gate. Then aim diagonally downhill, with the land dropping away on either side, towards the right-hand power pole on the road[12] ahead. Go across; follow the hedge on your left, and cross a bridge to arrive at the River Weaver[13].

River Weaver – Frodsham Hill (5.7 km, 3.6 mi):

Turn left[13] away from the river at the finger post, cross a stream and follow the field edge on your right to the road[12]. Go straight across and aim for a stile near an electricity pole at the highest point of the field ahead. Cross the stile, and aim for another in the direction of the houses on the far side of the next field. Cross the stile, bear slightly right to a waymark post[11] and stile in a new fence. Enter wood and zigzag down to a stream then up to a stile out of the wood. Turn right and cross the centre of the field to a fence and stile[10]. Cross, and then go left along the hedge to a stile on your left. Go over and follow the field edge to Hatley Farm, then along the farm road and over the first stile on your right[9].

Aim slightly left, with a pond on your left, over a stile, then diagonally across the next field to a stile in the far left corner. Go over and turn left along the hedge to Watery Lane[8]. Turn right, take the second path on your left[7] and follow the hedge on your left to the B5152[6]. Turn left and immediately right, then take the first road left. Take the first path to the right[5], bearing left across the field, keeping uphill of a bushy hollow, to a stile in the top right-hand corner. Go over and immediately turn right along the hedge with caves on your left. Follow the path sharp right along a hedge to Manley Road[4]. Turn left and first right (Simons Lane) to take the first path on your right[3]. Pass a cottage and then a hotel on your left, crossing the drive and then around the hillside to Bellemonte Road[2]. Turn left and then go through iron gates on the right to the war memorial on top of Frodsham Hill[1].

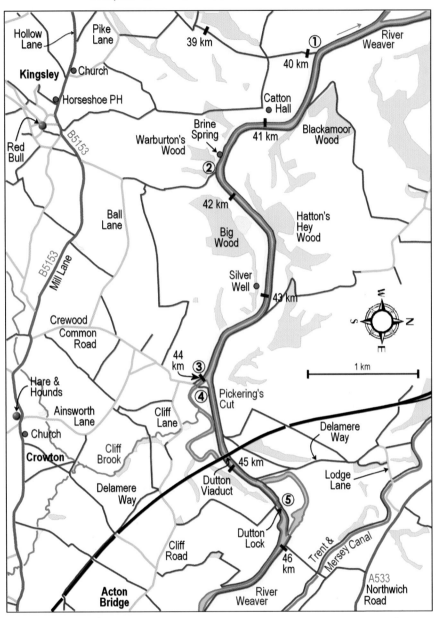

Numbers on the map refer to superscript numbers in the walking instructions

Chapter 4. River Weaver to Dutton Locks

River Weaver – Dutton Locks (5.5 km, 3.4 mi):

Turn right[1] (upstream) along the (left) bank of the River Weaver and follow it for almost 4 km with the river always on your left, ignoring any paths leading away from the river. On reaching a caravan park[3], enter through a small gate in a fence and follow the service road to the site entrance. Turn sharp left on the road, cross a footbridge and follow the path back to the river[4].

Turn right along the riverbank and follow it under Dutton railway viaduct and onto a boardwalk of railway sleepers. Continue along the riverbank to Dutton Locks[5]. Cross the locks and turn right along the other (right) bank of the river.

Dutton Locks – River Weaver (5.5 km, 3.4 mi):

Cross the locks[5] to the other (left) bank of the River Weaver and follow the riverbank downstream, passing under Dutton railway viaduct. 600m after the viaduct, where it becomes impossible to stay beside the river[4], take the path left.

Cross a footbridge to reach a road and almost immediately turn right into a caravan park[3]. Follow the service road through the park to a small fence and gate at the far end. Go through the gate and follow the path to the hedge corner and a kissing gate into a field. Turn right and follow the field boundary to reach the riverbank once more. Follow the riverbank; with the river always on your right and in 2¼ km ignore the side-path[2] climbing away from the river up a broad farm track. Just over 1½ km after this side-path, and after passing Catton Hall (farm and outbuildings converted to housing), leave the riverside at a finger post[1], going over a stile next to a field gate and following the hedge away from the river.

> ### Cheshire Dialect
> Cowshat – a wood pigeon
> Scharn – cow dung
> ... you'd think it might have been the other way round!

Dutton Locks

Frodsham to Dutton Locks – the Weaver Valley

The 11 km stretch of the North Cheshire Way from Frodsham to Dutton Locks presents a great variety of landscapes – starting high on the Cheshire Sandstone Ridge at Frodsham Hill, and then descending into the lower valley of the River Weaver. This eastern dip slope of the Sandstone Ridge is much gentler than the steep scarps of the western side and the northern end. Thus it is more populated, as Frodsham extends itself southwards into Overton, and the farmland becomes increasingly rich as the altitude decreases, the contours become more widely spaced and boulder clays enrich the sandy soils. Yet by the time the river valley is reached settlement is again sparser and we are back into a landscape of large dairy farms and lush grassland – the Cheshire Plain again. But here there is a difference … the valley of the River Weaver lies ahead.

The Weaver is the largest river actually encountered by the NCW and its lower valley is incised deep into the Cheshire Plain through the overlying boulder clay and into the underlying sandstone. The valley started life as a melt-water drainage channel beneath the ice age glaciers that carried silt, sand and boulders, which scoured out the valley. As the last ice age ended, the vigorous young river cut rapidly through the glacial deposits making a valley 30-60 metres (100-200 feet) deep. At the same time, its tributary streams cut deep steep-sided cloughs in the valley sides. Later, as the sea rose to flood the lower Mersey (then still out in the Irish Sea off Liverpool), the gradient of the river decreased and it flowed less rapidly. As a result, the river dropped much of the sediments it was carrying and thus the valley to a large extent refilled with sands and silts ("alluvium").

The part of the valley traversed by the NCW upstream towards Dutton Locks is still quite steep-sided. The river has cut its path into the sediments. The valley sides are well wooded and little streams descend through steep-sided wooded cloughs to join the main river. It is lowland river scenery at its best, – far from any town or village – and providing an attractive contrast between the riverside trail and the ancient woodland clothing the cloughs.

Nevertheless, much of what at first sight is an entirely natural landscape has in fact been wrought by man. The burgeoning growth of industry during the Industrial Revolution of the 18th and early 19th centuries led to the canalisation of the river, the navigable course being known as the "Weaver Navigation", to allow ocean-going vessels to penetrate from the Mersey to Northwich. The railways followed, and the river is crossed by the railway just before Dutton Locks by means of the spectacular Dutton Viaduct. The river is quieter nowadays with the decline in the chemical industry at Northwich and pleasure craft are as frequent as commercial traffic. This – and the absence of roads or settlements along the valley – has created an informal but beautiful linear nature reserve. Wild flowers are plentiful in their season, some of the clough and riverside woodland being quite ancient and species-rich, and bird life abounds.

Frodsham to Five Crosses: The NCW leaves the top of Frodsham Hill by a route that runs southwards, circling high on the east-facing slope of Frodsham and Beacon Hills. Here it briefly joins the Delamere Way. There are splendid views north and east to Runcorn with its chemical factories and twin road and rail bridges – the lowest crossing of the Mersey (other than by tunnel or ferry at Liverpool) – and the huge cooling towers of Fiddler's Ferry Power Station. To the south and east can be seen the Jodrell Bank radio telescope and the Pennines beyond. In the woods of Beacon Hill, right beside the NCW, is the Heathercliffe Hotel. This was at one time the home of John Paul Getty I, the oil tycoon, and later of Queen Alexandra of Yugoslavia (see box). More recently, it was used as a location for the filming of the TV film "Robin Hood" (1991).

Leaving Beacon Hill, the NCW goes past Frodsham Golf Club and soon reaches the "Hermit's Cave". Whether a hermit ever lived in these manmade sandstone caves is not known, but it is a more romantic thought than their former use as a source of sand for floors or their present use as cattle shelters. Nevertheless, this is a pretty spot when the gorse is in bloom. Onward then, to begin the descent of the east slope of the Sandstone Ridge and arrive at Five Crosses on the boundary between Frodsham to the north and Kingsley to the south.

> **Queen Alexandra of Yugoslavia**
>
> The most famous resident of what is now the Heathercliffe Hotel was Alexandra, last queen of Yugoslavia. Her story is a sad one. She was born in 1921 in Athens the posthumous daughter of Alexander I, King of the Hellenes (and cousin of Prince Philip, Duke of Edinburgh). In 1944, she married the exiled King Peter II of Yugoslavia, who was deposed by the new Communist regime only a year later. Her son Aleksandar Karađorđević remains pretender to the throne of Serbia. Alexandra died in England in 1993, never having set foot in Yugoslavia, and is buried in Greece.

Five Crosses to the River Weaver: After crossing the B5152, the NCW goes gently down the slope towards the river and through typical Cheshire Plain arable and dairy farmland. Just before we finally leave Frodsham the route is briefly shared with the Eddisbury Way before heading off to the east. After passing Hatley Farm a short detour north would lead to Bradley Hill Fort (marked as a "Settlement" on the OS map). This is the third of the trio of Iron Age forts along the northern end of the Sandstone Ridge and the least conspicuous. Most of the defences have been badly damaged by ploughing and disturbed by recent changes in field boundaries, but traces of the bank and ditch can still be made out from the nearby footpath. The final leg of this section is a further downhill journey – passing new housing at Belleair – to arrive on the banks of the Weaver just downstream of Catton Hall. This was once a country house but is now a centre for clay pigeon shooting, paintball, quad biking and archery – you have been warned!

Along the Weaver to Dutton Locks: from Catton Hall to Dutton Locks, the NCW follows the left bank of the Weaver, which has been straightened in places to ease navigation (the Weaver Navigation); sometimes the former meanders remain as reedy havens for wildlife. This is especially noticeable at Pickering's Cut and at Dutton Locks themselves.

The river itself is 50 miles long and rises at the foot of the Peckforton Hills much further south along the Sandstone Ridge. Work on the Weaver Navigation was started in 1730 and the last 20 miles of the river became open to navigation in 1732 with eleven locks (now only four) between Winsford and the Mersey at Runcorn. The main traffic was the carriage of salt

River Weaver near Well Wood

from the salt mines of mid-Cheshire and – in later years – chemicals from the former ICI works at Northwich. Pickering's Wharf, the former tidal limit prior to canalisation, was the transhipment point for salt and coal between boat and packhorse or wagon. "Foreign" grains – such as maize – were also taken from here by cart to Kingsley Mill. This became the site of one of the larger "cuts" and one of the original locks, now disappeared. Early records show even more varied cargoes – including cheese, onions, hops, ale … and gravestones! There is still a little commercial traffic, but the primary users are now pleasure boats, especially since the reopening of the Anderton Boat Lift (see Chapter 5). A further link with the salt industry is provided by the wild brine springs at the foot of the valley slopes – such as "Silver Well" – but these are hard to find.

The steep woodlands on either side of the river are largely unspoilt and have wild damsons, wild service trees and spindle trees and the rare small-leaved lime along with the more usual oak, ash, hazel, wych elm, wild cherry and blackthorn. The ground flora is also very rich and includes wood anemone, bluebell, primrose, yellow archangel, ramsons, bellflowers, violets and early purple orchids as well as several uncommon grasses, sedges and rushes. In the valley bottom, alder is dominant, together with sedges, marsh marigolds and bittersweet.

Chapter 4. Frodsham to Dutton Locks

Drier grassy areas by the river bank contain other species such as lousewort, knapweed, lady's mantle, betony and spotted orchid. The birdlife of the valley is also varied and includes great crested grebes, kestrels, kingfishers and herons – with buzzards often seen soaring overhead. Both Warburton's Wood and Well Wood are Sites of Special Scientific Interest (SSSIs) as prime examples of ancient semi-natural clough woodland. They occupy two deep cloughs and the steep bank of the Weaver, cutting through glacial sands and gravels and the older Bollin Mudstone Formation (formerly known as "Keuper marl").

Dutton Viaduct: Just downstream of Dutton locks the Weaver is crossed by the West Coast Main Line Railway (originally the Grand Junction Railway, opened in 1837). The railway spans the river by the twenty arches of the Dutton Viaduct, 460 metres long and standing 18 metres above the river with exceptionally wide (18 metre) spans. It was built in 1837 by Joseph Locke from designs

Dutton Viaduct

by George Stephenson to complete the rail link from Birmingham to Manchester and Liverpool. Many tons of cotton waste were used in the foundations to give the structure resilience when trains passed over.

Dutton Locks: *(Illustration on page 49).* The end of this sector of the NCW is at Dutton Locks – the first crossing point of the river upstream of Frodsham, now that Pickering's Lock has disappeared. This is a beautiful spot and is well appointed with picnic tables. There are also some interesting sculptures, including one in wood of the "Elizabeth", a Weaver flat (a double-ended square-sailed boat, adapted from those used at the time on the Mersey). The present locks were built in 1874 of Runcorn sandstone, Derbyshire limestone and Cornish granite. The larger of the twin locks measures 67 x 13 metres with a 2.4 metre rise. The brick-built lock-tenders' cottages remain beside the locks.

Nearby Trails and Places to Visit

Eddisbury Way: Meets the NCW in Bradley. It is a waymarked route created and maintained by The Mid-Cheshire Footpath Society and runs for 26 km (18 miles) from Frodsham to the Sandstone Trail at Burwardsley.

Lady Heyes Craft Centre: On the B5152 between Frodsham and Kingsley. Craft centre and tea rooms – including the Cheshire Book Centre.

Warburton's Wood: Nature reserve, owned and managed by Cheshire Wildlife Trust. Access from Ball Lane, off the B5153 east of Kingsley (800 metre walk from parking area). SSSI with distinctive flora (see above).

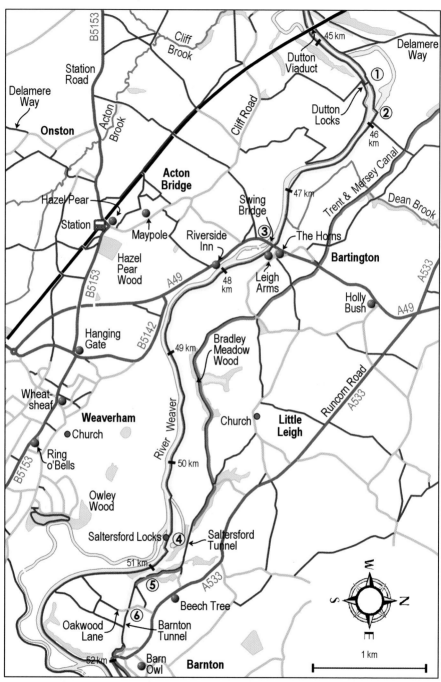

Numbers on the map refer to superscript numbers in the walking instructions

Chapter 5. Dutton Locks to Barnton

Dutton Locks – Barnton (5.9 km, 3.7 mi):

Cross the River Weaver at Dutton Locks[1] and continue with the canalised river on your right, soon crossing a bridge[2] over the old river above a weir. Continue along the service road beside the river for almost 2 km to the black and white swing bridge[3] that carries the A49 main road over the river. Go under the bridge and keep to the riverside path for just over 3 km to Saltersford Locks[4]. Pass in front of a cottage and follow the road. In about 300m, take the road uphill and away from the river to reach the Trent & Mersey Canal[5]. Turn right and walk with the canal on your left. In 200m the canal disappears into Saltersford Tunnel; keep straight ahead on the old horse road and in 200m arrive at a crossroads[6] with Oakwood Lane, Barnton.

Barnton – Dutton Locks (5.9 km, 3.7 mi):

Go straight over the crossroads[6] at Oakwood Lane, Barnton, and descend the road to the Trent & Mersey Canal as it emerges from Saltersford Tunnel. Continue with the canal on your right for 200m and then leave the canal[5], following the road down to the River Weaver below. Turn right alongside the river to Saltersford Locks[4], passing the keeper's cottage on your right. Follow the riverside path, with the river always on your left, for just over 3 km to reach the black and white swing bridge[3] carrying the A49 main road across the river. Go under the road and continue beside the river for almost 2 km. Soon after crossing a bridge[2] over the old course of the river, above a weir, you will arrive at Dutton Locks[1].

Trent & Mersey Canal between Saltersford and Barnton tunnels

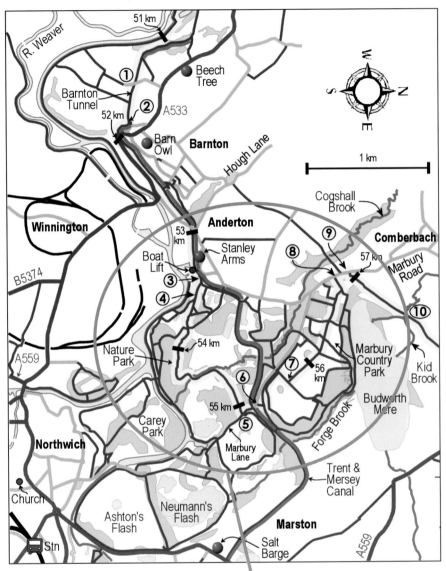

Numbers on the map refer to superscript numbers in the walking instructions

See page 58 for more detail
on Marbury Country Park

Chapter 5. Barnton to Budworth Mere

Barnton – Budworth Mere (6.1 km, 3.8 mi):

Go straight over the cross roads[1] at Oakwood Lane and downhill to rejoin the towpath as the canal emerges from Barnton Tunnel[2]. Do not cross the canal. Follow the towpath, with the canal on your left for 1½ km to the Anderton Boat Lift. After the information centre bear right[3] away from the canal with picnic tables on your left. At the top, cross to the car park with the vehicular entrance to your left to avoid traffic. Go around the right-hand edge of the car park and exit by the Dragonfly Gate[4]. Continue, with the river below to the right, to a 4-way finger post. Go straight ahead, crossing the brook at Lesley's Leap and on reaching Marbury Lane[5], go left. Cross the canal and take the first path on the right[6] into the woods. Take the first turning sharp left at a 3-way finger post and in 340m go right on a track across grassland. In 120m go left at a finger post[7] (signed 'car park'). After the lime tree avenue go straight ahead, passing public conveniences on your right, to a T-junction. Turn left past the garden centre to Marbury Road[8]. Go right on the road for 150m and take the first footpath on your right[9]. Bear left across the field, soon with woods on your right, and follow a fence on the left to the footbridge over Kid Brook[10].

Budworth Mere – Barnton (6.1 km, 3.8 mi):

Cross the footbridge[10] over Kid Brook, continue with a fence on your right and keep to the same direction across a field to Marbury Road[9]. In 150m, go left at the nursery entrance[8] and in 130m go right on a footpath across the remains of Marbury Hall, passing public conveniences on your left. Go straight ahead down the lime tree avenue. At the end of the next field go right at a finger post[7] and in 120m bear left along a footpath through woods (*ignore the broader track that turns left at the same point; this is for cyclists and riders and soon turns in the wrong direction*). In 340m, at a 3-way finger post, go sharp right (not ahead towards the canal) to a stile onto Marbury Lane[6]. Turn left across the canal, go through a gate and then take the path to the right[5] (signed 'Uplands Woods'). Continue on the main path, crossing the brook at Lesley's Leap, to a 4-way finger post. Keep straight ahead to the Dragonfly Gate[4] and then go around the left-hand edge of the car park. At the far side, cross the road (with the vehicular entrance to your right to avoid the traffic) and bear left down to the towpath[3], past picnic tables on your right. Go left, pass the Anderton Boat Lift, and follow the towpath for 1½ km. Where the canal disappears into Barnton Tunnel[2] go up a cobbled path, bearing left past a house and follow the old horse track to the crossroads[1] at Oakwood Lane.

> **Cheshire Dialect**
> Gilhooter – an owl
> Shepstir – a starling

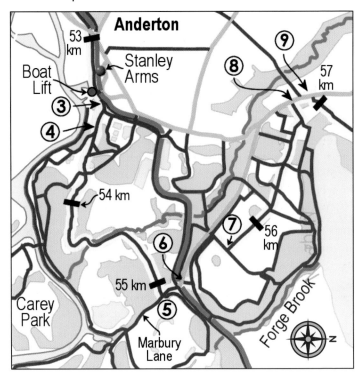

North Cheshire Way through Marbury Country Park

The Salt of the Earth

The oceans cover over 70% of the earth's surface and contain 97% of the water on earth. And this ocean water is 3.5% salt – as is human blood, perhaps reflecting our marine origins as a species. Without salt we could not live and all of the salt we use comes ultimately from the oceans. No mineral is more used, or has more uses – and salt is the "white gold" of Cheshire. In the Triassic period, 200-250 million years ago, Cheshire was near the equator and much of the county was covered by a shallow lake, which evaporated in the tropical sun creating vast deposits of salt. This has made Cheshire the source of 85% of Britain's salt, some 6 million tons a year, used for de-icing roads, in the food industry and – about two-thirds of the total – in the chemical industry. As a raw material, salt is the source of chlorine – key to many aspects of modern everyday life – for example, 85% of all medicines and the purification of 98% of European drinking water.

Salt's preservative ability was a foundation of civilization as it reduced man's dependence on the seasonal availability of food and allowed him to travel long distances. In fact, it was so highly valued that until the 1900s, salt was one of the prime movers of national economies and wars – and thus was taxed from as far back as the 20th century BC! Even the word "salary", upon which we so much depend (!), comes from the Latin "*salarium*" implying payment in salt. In a very real sense, salt still underlies Cheshire … and its economy.

Dutton Locks to Budworth Mere – the Story of Salt

From Dutton Locks to Budworth Mere the NCW runs for 12 km through the Weaver valley. At first, it runs along the north bank of the River Weaver, then along the Trent and Mersey Canal, skirting the ancient salt town of Northwich. It continues through Anderton Nature Park and Marbury Country Park to reach the fields running down to Budworth Mere. For the walker, the natural beauty of the valley forms a counterpoint to the industrial archaeology of a region rich in the history of canals and of the chemical industry. Above all this is salt country, where many aspects of today's landscape find their origins in the vast tropical lake that covered the area over 200 million years ago, whose evaporation created the thick beds of rock salt, up to 280 metres (900 feet) thick and between 100 and 250 metres (350 to 800 feet) underground.

Salt production in mid-Cheshire goes back to the Iron Age and was widespread in Roman times. Brine from natural salt springs was heated in earthenware or lead pans to produce salt crystals. By the Middle Ages, the industry was regulated to a degree that seems familiar in today's bureaucratic world. There were rules governing the number of "wich" houses producing salt, the number of salt pans one person could own and even the seasons and hours when salt-making could be carried out. The introduction of coal firing and iron pans in the 18th century greatly increased production – and also greatly depleted the woodlands of the Cheshire forest of Mare and Mondrum.

Historically, salt was won by mining of "rock salt" or by pumping "wild brine" to access the natural brine trapped at the top of the underground deposits where rainwater was slowly dissolving the rock salt. But there were unwanted side effects. The flooding of old shallow mine workings or the collapse of the overlying strata due to uncontrolled pumping of wild brine led to much subsidence in the area. Many buildings in Northwich are of timber-frame construction so that they could be jacked up or even moved when the ground collapsed beneath them. Millions of tons of fly ash are now being injected into the old mines beneath Northwich to stabilise them and allow regeneration of the town.

Now only one salt mine remains – near Winsford, south of Northwich. Most salt is now "solution mined" by controlled pumping of water underground to dissolve the salt with the resulting brine pumped back to the surface. The size and shape of the resulting cavities are carefully controlled to avoid subsidence.

Dutton Locks to Saltersford Locks: The River Weaver may justifiably be called a "salt" water; when it opened to navigation in 1732, almost 80% of the recorded cargo on the river was salt! From Dutton Locks, the NCW follows the riverbank to Acton Bridge. Here, the A49 main road crosses by a swing bridge, allowing ships to pass upstream to Northwich. The valley widens out upstream of the locks with fields either side of the river used for mixed farming. The steep valley sides have receded and – especially on the right (north) bank – can be seen, clad in their characteristic woodland, across the fields. There is little settlement along the river, except for the hamlet of Bartington (in the Domesday Book, but now almost "lost") near the swing bridge. The main village centres are set back a mile or two on the higher land, where orchards of apples and pears add to the usual mixed farming. Acton Bridge was famed for its "hazel pear" trees, (also known as "hessle pears", from Hessle near Hull, or – locally – as "toadbacks" from their extensive russet spotting). Weaverham is a large village, once famous for its Russet apples – making a pair (should that be "pear"?) with Acton Bridge. Back on the NCW, we arrive at Saltersford Locks, where the mediaeval salt traders crossed the river. This is the beginning of the "Barnton Cut" built between 1832 and 1835 to improve navigation.

Trent and Mersey Canal: Shortly after Saltersford Locks, the NCW says goodbye to the Weaver and climbs up the valley side to the Trent and Mersey Canal, now running closely parallel to the river but some 20 metres above it. Also known as the "Grand Trunk Canal", the Trent and Mersey opened in sections between 1770 and 1777 and is one of the earliest of the English canals. It runs for 93 miles from the Bridgewater Canal at Preston Brook, near Runcorn, to Shardlow on the River Trent in the Midlands. It was built by James Brindle for the "captains of industry" in the Potteries to bring flint and china clay from the Mersey, coal from Lancashire and to carry their wares to Manchester and Birmingham. Today it is a leisure cruising route, forming a link between the west and east coasts of England. The NCW follows the towpath of the canal with views across the Weaver to the nearby "salt town" of Northwich.

Barnton: Soon after we join the canal, it plunges through the 520 metre Barnton Tunnel, leaving us to climb the old horse track over the top. The village grew as a dormitory for the works at Northwich across the river. It lies above the canal, which in turn lies above the river on the far bank of which are the large Brunner Mond soda ash plants that use Cheshire salt

Barnton Tunnel

as a key raw material. The canal towpath presents us with a quite different world – shaded by trees, there are ducks and other waterfowl and the occasional coruscating blue of a passing kingfisher.

Chapter 5. Dutton Locks to Budworth Mere

Anderton Boat Lift: The NCW continues along the towpath to Anderton, where we find the Anderton Boat Lift, known as the "cathedral of the canals". When the Trent and Mersey Canal opened in 1777, Anderton was the transhipment point for goods to the Weaver Navigation 15 metres below. They were moved by a combination of inclined planes and chutes. A hundred years later, the trustees of the Weaver Navigation commissioned a "boat carrying lift" that was designed by Edward Leader  Williams (who went on to build the Manchester Ship Canal) and Edwin Clark. The original lift, the world's first, was completed in 1875. It had two caissons, each capable of carrying two canal narrow-boats. The caissons were supported on hydraulic rams and the lift operated hydraulically with steam assistance. It suffered severely from corrosion by the canal water used as the hydraulic fluid and in 1908 was replaced by a new lift on the same site. This time the two counterbalanced caissons were raised and lowered by wire ropes and pulleys, assisted by a small electric motor. The new lift remained in use until 1982 when mechanical problems again forced its closure. After a £7 million pound renovation programme, it reopened as a tourist attraction, restoring the link for leisure craft between canal and river and is now Britain's only working boat lift.

Anderton Nature Park: After the boat lift, the NCW leaves the canal and climbs up into Anderton Nature Park. This is part of the Northwich Community Woodlands, which is part of Mersey Forest. The woodlands are part of plans to improve the local environment of Northwich by restoring many of the semi-derelict industrial sites as nature reserves and for leisure use.

Much of the park occupies an area of large "lagoons" that were used for dumping lime-rich wastes from the soda ash industry in the early 1900s. This left a lime-rich environment, unusual in Cheshire whose soils are mostly sands and clays. This supports a characteristic flora, including species rare or absent in the rest of the county. For example, there are a number of orchid species, along with creeping willow, traveller's joy, bird's-foot trefoil, teasel and weld. There is also a natural salt marsh flora, including wild celery and sea spurge. Other more generally distributed Cheshire species also abound, such as figwort, willow-herbs, wild angelica, violets, hawthorn, bramble and dog rose. The lagoons have been allowed to re-flood and now form an important breeding and wintering site for wildfowl.

After the visitor car park, the NCW passes through the sculptured "Dragonfly Gate" – a reminder that the park is also species-rich in invertebrates, particularly the dragonflies and damselflies that frequent the many small pools and also butterflies and moths – including the rare dingy skipper. The NCW goes on through Anderton Nature Park and crosses the wooded clough of Marbury Brook at Lesley's Leap, where kingfishers can be seen, before reaching Marbury Lane and crossing our old friend the Trent and Mersey Canal.

Marbury Country Park: After the canal, the NCW enters Marbury Country Park, part of Northwich Community Woodlands. The original Marbury Hall was the home of the Smith-Barry family, one of the great Cheshire land-owning families, who intermarried and had country houses at Arley, Tabley and Tatton. The new hall, built around 1840, was pulled down in 1968 after years of dereliction. An old ice house and avenues of limes planted in the 1840s survive. Terraces lead down to Budworth Mere. The park was used during World War II as a German prisoner-of-war camp and the site of an unsuccessful escape attempt – four POWs were recaptured at the controls of a bomber at the American airfield at Burtonwood! After the war the park housed many Polish people displaced by the hostilities. Later still it was used by ICI for workers awaiting housing during the post-war period of austerity. The Hall and surrounding woods are said to be haunted.

The White Lady of Marbury

Earl Barrymore of Marbury Hall, while a young man visiting the Pyramids and Sphinx, fell in love with a beautiful dark-haired Egyptian girl. He brought her back to Marbury and they spent an idyllic English summer there beside the mere. But the girl passed away in the chill of the first winter, her dying wish to be mummified and buried where she had been happiest so that she would never have to leave Marbury Hall. Eventually the young man married and all was peaceful until a later generation, embarrassed by their ancestor's adventure outside of the bonds of wedlock, tried to have her re-interred in Great Budworth churchyard. Then the White Lady appeared as the girl's heart-broken spirit came back to remonstrate with the all-too-Victorian family – and only ceased to haunt the Hall when her coffin was disinterred and brought back there. Eventually the family died out, childless, and the Hall fell into dereliction. The coffin is still buried there, but the restless spirit of this daughter of Aida is still said to haunt the woods and the hollows along Marbury Lane. Walkers are advised to proceed with caution – especially after dark.

Chapter 5. Dutton Locks to Budworth Mere

The Park is now managed by the County Council as a country park with walks and cycle trails, lime avenues, ancient woodland, open parkland, a small arboretum and terraces with glimpses of Budworth Mere. Birch and oak woodlands support a variety of bird life, including all three British woodpeckers, as well as typical Cheshire woodland flora – bluebells, wood anemones, dog's mercury and wood sorrel. The arboretum, just south of the NCW, was designed and planted in Victorian times when the new hall was built. Among the more unusual species are grand firs, red cedars, and the deodar cedar – as well as Turkey oaks and their cross with the cork oak, the evergreen Luccombe Oak with its unusual corky bark. An orchard with local varieties of apples and damsons was added in 1995.

Budworth Mere: Leaving Marbury Park behind, the NCW finally resumes a northeasterly direction and heads out across fields, descending to Kid Brook near where it enters Budworth Mere. The Cheshire Plain has many meres, some formed as deep depressions within deposits of glacial moraine, while others arose more recently by subsidence as a result of the extraction of salt. It is not entirely clear which is the origin of Budworth Mere. The mere is the haunt of the grebe and heron, curlew and sandpiper. Although the NCW does not reach the shores of the mere, there are excellent views across the water to the village of Great Budworth beyond. But that must await another chapter …

Nearby Trails and Places to Visit

Cheshire Ring Canal Walk: This route is shared with the NCW along the Trent and Mersey Canal between Barnton and Anderton. It is a 156 km (98 mile) circular route following the Trent and Mersey, Bridgewater, Rochdale, Ashton, Peak Forest and Macclesfield Canals – the "Cheshire Ring".

Delamere Way: Crosses the NCW at Dutton Locks. It is a waymarked route created and maintained by The Mid-Cheshire Footpath Society and runs for 34 km (21 miles) from Frodsham via Delamere Forest to Stockton Heath.

Lion Salt Works, Marston: On the B5075, just north of Northwich. Britain's only remaining open-pan salt works.

Northwich: Just south of the NCW lies the salt town of Northwich, now undergoing regeneration from a largely industrial past. The Salt Museum in the old workhouse in London Road is well worth a visit. The town bridge over the Weaver is not only a swing bridge to allow vessels to pass; it is a *floating* swing bridge, on pontoons to cope with subsidence! There are good services for walkers – accommodation, refreshment, shops and good transport links. The station is on the Manchester to Chester line, while nearby Hartford station (3½ km / 2 miles) lies on the London to Liverpool main line.

Chapter 6. Budworth Mere to Arley

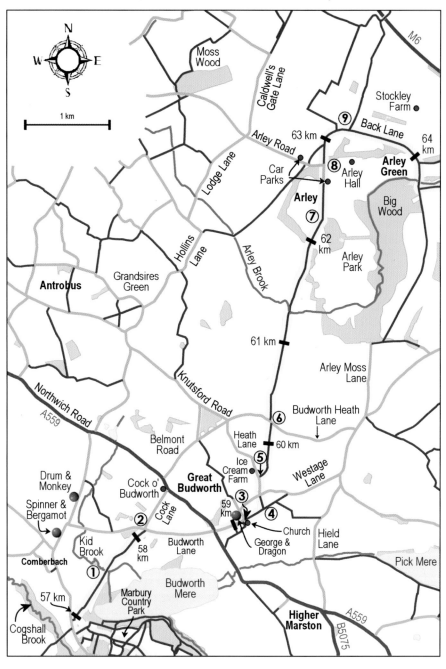

Numbers on the map refer to superscript numbers in the walking instructions

64

Budworth Mere – Arley (5.7 km, 3.6 mi):

Cross the bridge[1] over Kid Brook and keep the fence on your left until you can see the way into the wood ahead. Go through the wood to reach Budworth Lane[2]. Turn right on the lane to the A559 main road and go straight across into Great Budworth village. Where the road turns left[3], keep straight ahead down a little lane to the left of the church. In 200m, at the end of an avenue of big trees, turn left[4] down a lane with houses to reach the road at a junction. Go straight across, down Heath Lane. At a finger post[5] just before New Westage Farm ("ice cream farm") go over a stile on the right and follow the edge of the field, keeping the fence on your right. Go over a stile, crossing a farm track and two further stiles, and then keep the field boundary on your left until you reach a lane[6]. Cross the lane and take the metalled drive to the left of the farm; this eventually becomes a concrete farm track and then a footpath. Keep straight ahead for 1 km, with the field boundaries always on your right, to a stile into a small copse. In the copse go right over either of two bridges across Arley Brook then immediately left, exit the copse and again keep straight ahead for 1 km, with boundaries always on your right, until the path reaches the metalled Arley estate road[7]. Turn left on the road and keep straight ahead passing car parks and the main entrance to Arley Hall[8]. Do not turn left here onto Arley Road, but keep straight ahead (north) onto Back Lane. Ignore all paths to the left and follow the broad lane as it gradually turns right to circle the Arley estate[9].

Arley – Budworth Mere (5.7 km, 3.6 mi):

Continue along Back Lane[9], ignoring all paths to the right, to reach the road junction at the main entrance to Arley Hall[8]. Keep straight ahead on the estate road, passing car parks on either side. Just after reaching woods on the left, at a finger post[7], take the path bearing off into fields on the right. Go straight ahead for 1 km, always keeping the field boundaries on your left, until you reach a gate into a small copse. In the copse go right over either of two bridges across Arley Brook and immediately left to leave the copse by a stile. Continue straight ahead for 1 km, with field boundaries to the left, as the footpath becomes a concrete farm track and eventually a metalled drive. On reaching the public road[6], go straight across and over a stile. Keep the fence on your right to reach two stiles onto a farm track. Cross the track and go over the stile opposite, then follow the field edge ahead and then right to reach Heath Lane[5]. New Westage Farm ("ice cream farm") is visible just off the route on your right. Turn left and at the T-junction keep straight ahead down a track. In 130m turn right at the next path[4] and pass the school and church to meet the road[3]. Go straight ahead, away from the church, and on reaching the A559 main road go straight across and up Budworth Lane. Continue to the junction with Cock Lane on your right. Here take the footpath on the left[2] into woods. Go through the wood and exit into fields, bearing right towards a fence. On reaching the fence bear left and continue with it on your right to reach the footbridge[1] over Kid Brook.

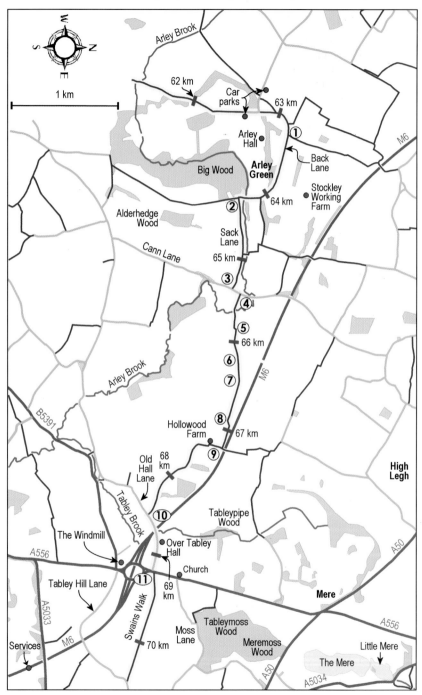

Numbers on the map refer to superscript numbers in the walking instructions

Chapter 6. Arley to Tabley

Arley – Tabley (5.9 km, 3.7 ml):

Continue along Back Lane[1], passing the picturesque houses and former school at Arley Green. Shortly after passing a small lake on the right, turn left at a path crossing[2] and continue along Sack Lane for 1 km to reach Cann Lane[3].

Go left on the lane for 100m and take the next path on the right[4]. Follow the former hedge-line, indicated by two or three trees, to a footbridge over Arley Brook. Cross and follow the hedge on the right to the end of the next field, then turn left for 30m to a stile and sandstone slab bridge[5] over a ditch. Cross and go straight across the next field to a stile onto a farm track[6].

Go straight across the track and over another stile into a very large field. Aim for the left-hand edge of a clump of large trees[7] surrounding ponds and in 230m, at a finger post, go slightly right across the rest of the field for 460m to a stile in the hedge[8]. Go over the stile, and bear left across the field corner for 60m to another stile. Now angle slightly towards the M6 motorway on your left to reach the boundary fence where the power lines cross overhead, and then follow the fence to a footbridge over the M6. Do not cross the bridge, but turn right[9] away from the motorway towards Hollowood Farm.

Go through the farmyard with the house on your right and barns on your left and then continue for a further 1.1 km down the lane to the junction with Old Hall Lane[10]. Turn left, cross the motorway and continue to the T-junction[11] with the A556 near the roundabout at Over Tabley.

Tabley – Arley (5.9 km, 3.7 ml):

Turn right[11] from the A556 down Old Hall Lane, cross the M6 motorway and take the next turning right[10] (signed 'No Through Road'). Go down this lane for 1.1 km and on approaching Hollowood Farm take the right hand (lesser) fork towards farm buildings.

Go through the farmyard, leave it through two gates and go along the field edge to reach a footbridge over the M6. Do not cross the bridge, but turn left[9] beside the fence. On reaching overhead power lines bear slightly left and away from the M6 to a stile in the hedge. Cross and bear left for 60m to a further stile[8]. Cross into a very large field, aiming towards a clump of trees[7] 460m away beside ponds. Leave the trees on your left and at a finger post bear slightly left for a further 230m to a stile onto a farm track[6].

Go straight across the track and over another stile. Go ahead across the field, still bearing slightly away from the M6, to a concealed ditch crossing[5] of sandstone slabs and a stile some 320m away and just to the right of a hedge corner. Cross the stile and immediately turn left along the hedge to the field corner, then turn right, keeping the hedge on your left. Cross the footbridge over Arley Brook, then bear slightly right following a line of trees to a stile onto Cann Lane[4]. Turn left for 100m and then right at the rhyming signpost[3] (for Arley Hall) onto Sack Lane.

Go straight down the lane for 1 km, and then turn right at a path crossing[2] (where the way ahead is a private entrance to the Arley estate). Pass a lake on the left to reach the cottages and old school at Arley Green. Continue ahead along Back Lane[1], which soon becomes cobbled, with fields on the right and the Arley estate on the left.

Cheshire Dialect
Edther bowt – a dragonfly
Forkin Robin – an earwig

Budworth Mere to Tabley – to the Manor Born

From the footbridge across Kid Brook, the NCW runs for just under 12 km to Over Tabley across a rural northern part of the Cheshire Plain. This is rich and peaceful countryside, a dairy farming landscape with fields put down to grass for grazing, hay or silage. Parkland estates remain, where the farmland is varied by planted woodland and large specimen trees. Pastures are often neatly set behind black and white metal rail fences known as "Cheshire Railings"; these were introduced by Cheshire County Council for livestock control and subsequently adopted nationwide. Quintessentially English in character, this is a rural scene that seems a thousand miles from the cities, or from the toils and turmoil of Westminster. Despite the changes wrought by the modern management of the farms, this is still terrain redolent of a half-forgotten land – the England of the school on the village green, the huntsman in scarlet, the parson and the squire, the village pub – and country folk living out their lives to the unchanging rhythm of the seasons. Politicians agonise over the loss of a sense of what it is to be English: they should walk the North Cheshire Way and perhaps blow away some of the cobwebs that hide the memory of what was, to some extent still is – and still might be. This remains a green and pleasant land as we leave behind the railways, canals and industry of the Northwich area and enjoy a quieter interlude before more closely approaching the towns that lie further east.

Budworth Mere to Great Budworth: Leaving Kid Brook, the NCW climbs up through a small bluebell wood to Budworth Lane. Away from the trail to the west, lies the village of Comberbach, whose lands once belonged to the Knights of St. John of Jerusalem. This is a small rural village where the centuries-old farming community has been joined by commuters who value the peace and quiet of a retreat from their workaday lives. The village mummers still perform and meet – in the local pub, of course! After a short stretch along a lane with views of the mere, the route arrives in the village of Great Budworth.

Great Budworth: This is a picture-book English village of red brick and timber-framed cottages standing with twisted chimneys beside cobblestone pavements, clustering around an ancient church on a green hill overlooking Budworth and Pick Meres. Entering the village from the west, the NCW passes the Dene Well on a shady corner where the village street climbs up from the old turnpike road. The Dene stream for centuries fed the "Running Pump", the only water source for the village until 1890 and in use until 1932. The well house was built in 1869 and restored in 2003.

The 'Running Pump', Great Budworth

The street climbs up past picturesque cottages where the sharp-eyed may spot the inscription above three of them that taken together reads: *"Take thy calling thankfullie. Love thy neighbor neighborlie. Shun the path to beggarie"*. Soon the NCW arrives at the centre of village – defined by some perhaps as the church, by others as the pub opposite.

The church of St. Mary and All Saints dates back to Norman times and was for centuries closely associated with the Canons of Norton Priory, near Runcorn (on the Mersey some 12 km to the northwest). The present buildings date mostly from the 14th and 15th centuries and, like so much in and around this village, greatly benefited from the philanthropy of the Lord of the Manor, Rowland Warburton of Arley Hall who financed its restoration in the mid-19th century. Outside the church are the village stocks. Perhaps these are for those who imbibed too freely at the ivy-clad "George and Dragon" opposite, where the apt inscription above the porch reads: *"As Saint George in armed array did the fiery dragon slay, so mayst thou, with might no less, slay that dragon drunkenness"*. Nonetheless, the pub seems to do a good trade.

Great Budworth to Arley: As we leave the village, there is a final temptation to pause – at New Westage Farm, better known locally as "the ice cream farm", which in season often hosts a "maize maze". Walkers elsewhere in rural Cheshire will be well accustomed to less official (and less legal) versions of the latter where paths cross unreinstated maize fields through crops well above their heads. The route now goes on through fields for some distance, crossing Arley Brook to arrive at Arley with its Hall and Green.

Arley: Here in the parish of Aston-by-Budworth, Arley Hall has been the home of the Warburton family since the time of "Wise Piers" Warburton in

Arley Hall, from the park

Chapter 6. Budworth Mere to Tabley

1469 and the lands owned by them for longer. In the 19th century the hall passed to Rowland Eyles Egerton-Warburton, one of the Egertons of Oulton Park, who with his wife Mary had the house rebuilt between 1832 and 1845 in Victorian Jacobean stile, replacing an earlier timber-framed construction. They also laid out much of the present gardens. Still a private home, the Hall is occasionally open for special events but it is the gardens that are the big tourist attraction bringing in 30,000 visitors a year. The gardens overlook the beautiful park and are famed for their double herbaceous border – although the maze and bowling green have disappeared. There is also a large private chapel designed by Anthony Salvin (perhaps best known in Cheshire for his Peckforton Castle on the sandstone ridge further south). The site is used from time to time as a film location – for productions ranging from Galsworthy's "Forsyte Saga" to "Coronation Street". One wonders what would "Wise Piers" have thought.

Rowland Egerton-Warburton, the 19th century squire, was an English country gentleman to the hilt. He was the Lord of the Manor, Deputy Lieutenant of Cheshire, Justice of the Peace, a great benefactor to the local community – and, of course, a dedicated huntsman. As if all of this were not enough, he was also a prolific minor poet – publishing both under his own name and under the pseudonym of "Rambling Richard". Much of his work reflected his love of history, horses and hunting – and his "Hunting Songs" represent both a large part of his work and a rich source of Cheshire folk history. When blindness afflicted him in old age, he resorted to creating the numerous rhymes that adorn buildings and finger posts throughout the estate. We have already encountered the "temperance couplet" at the "George and Dragon" in Great Budworth.

> Then what a power o' gentlefolk did I set oies upon!
> A reining in their hunters, aw blood 'orses every one!
> They'd aw got bookskin leathers on, a fitten 'em so toight,
> As roind an plump as turmits be, an just about as whoit;
> Their spurs wor maid o' siller, and their buttons maid o' brass,
> Their coats wor red as carrots an their collurs green as grass.
>
> *Farmer Dobbin. A Day wi' the Cheshur Fox Dugs*
> *Rowland Eyles Egerton-Warburton, 1853*
> *(A description of a meet, in his version of Cheshire dialect!)*

Beyond the hall, and passing the squire's rhyming reminder that the route is a bridleway not a road (*"No Cartway, save on sufferance, here. For Horse and Foot the Road is clear To Lymm, High Legh, Hoe Green, & Mere"*), the NCW arrives at the little settlement of Arley Green. This is a picture-postcard scene that looks too perfectly English to be real. The green with its spreading oak tree, the little Victorian village school, a few ivy-clad slate-roofed red brick houses with their crazy spiral chimney pots, the red letterbox and the small lake fed by Arley Brook at the bottom of the green. All it needs is the maypole that once saw annual use (after chapel at nine o'clock … harmoniously melding Christian and pagan tradition).

Arley to Tabley: Departing Arley Green, the route leaves Arley Park by Sack Lane and at the junction with Cann Lane passes the last of the rhyming finger posts (*"This Road forbidden is to all, Unless they wend their way to call At Mill or Green or Arley Hall"*). The way ahead now lies across fields typical of the Cheshire Plain. The soil is heavier here and fields of wheat, maize and turnips lie between sheep and cattle pasture. Soon we converge with the M6 motorway – a rude awakening to remind us that we are back in the 21st century – and arrive in the parish of Tabley Superior, dating back to the Domesday Book and retaining the Latin form in its administrative title, although the settlement has adopted the vernacular and calls itself Over Tabley. On our route, we pass by Over Tabley Hall (now being converted into modern apartments) just before we arrive beside the huge roundabout at junction 19 of the M6 and the end of this part of the North Cheshire Way.

Nearby Trails and Places to Visit

Pick Mere: Sister lake to Budworth Mere – informal recreational open space with tree planting and bird life (reed warblers, barn owls); also water sports.

Stockley Working Farm: A modern working dairy farm on 700 acres of Cheshire farmland on the Arley Estate (access by tractor shuttle from the Arley car park). Farm animals (including 1500 Holstein/Friesian dairy cows), lamb feeding, birds of prey, farm trail, adventure play area, pond dipping and – of course – a chance to watch the milking.

Arley Green

Chapter 7. Tabley to Shaw Heath

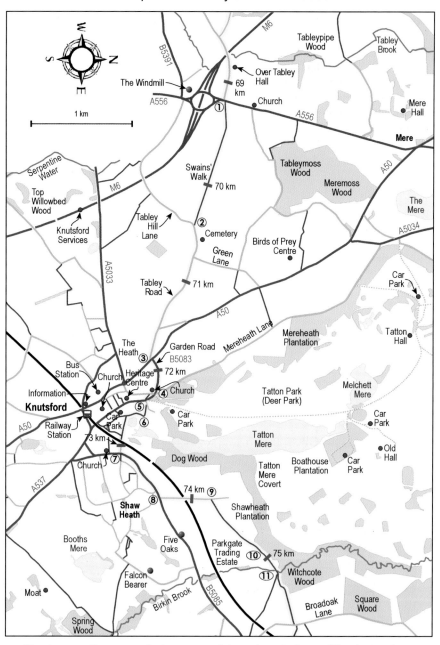

Numbers on the map refer to superscript numbers in the walking instructions

Chapter 7. Tabley to Shaw Heath

Tabley – Shaw Heath (6.0 km, 3.8 mi):

Cross the A556 Chester Road[1] with care, using the central refuge, and enter the farm entrance opposite to follow the bridleway (Swain's Walk) straight ahead for 1.25 km to Tabley Road[2]. Go left, crossing the road as soon as there is a footway on the other side, and continue to the A50 Manchester Road[3]. Cross over and keep straight ahead into Garden Road. At the 5-way junction[4] by St Vincent de Paul church go right (Tatton Street), passing in front of the church, cross the road and go half-right across the middle of the small green space opposite to emerge on King Street.

Cross the road and go straight ahead downhill with the Ruskin Reading Room[5] on the right. Keep to the right, directly in front of the buildings, down Drury Lane; at the bottom of the hill go right[6] along an unadopted road (Moorside) with the mere on your left. At the end of the mere go left beside the mere and then straight ahead under the railway and up Middle Walk to the B5085 Mobberley Road[7]. Go left and follow the road for 600m. Just after the fire station go left into Parkgate Lane[8].

Cross the railway and keep straight ahead for 280m, passing the GPO distribution centre at Haig Road. Then go right over a stile[9] onto a footpath that at first follows the hedge on the right beside the Parkgate Trading Estate. After 230m the path leaves the hedge and strikes out diagonally across horse paddocks with squeeze stiles – aim for an oak tree and then for the far left corner of the field where there is a stile beside the wood[10]. Go over the stile and follow the edge of the wood until it veers off to the left to form a recessed field corner. Keep straight ahead here across the field and descend steeply to the bridge and stile over Birkin Brook[11].

Shaw Heath – Tabley (6.0 km, 3.8 mi):

Cross the bridge and stile over Birkin Brook[11] and bear slightly left up the bank to the woodland boundary that converges from the right. Follow the edge of the wood to a stile[10] in the field corner and cross into a very large field. After passing two ponds look for a dead tree between two oaks in the distance. Aim for the left-hand oak, which is close to the edge of the Parkgate Trading Estate. As you approach the buildings go through a series of squeeze stiles across horse paddocks and on reaching the hedge turn right and follow it to a stile[9] onto Parkgate Lane.

Turn left and follow the lane over the railway to the B5085 Mobberley Road[8]. Turn right and continue to a controlled pedestrian crossing, turning right[7] here down Middle Walk and under the railway. Keep straight ahead with the mere on your right and at the end turn right onto an unadopted road (Moorside) with mere still on your right. At the end[6], turn away from the lake up Drury Lane until it merges with Highgate Road at the Ruskin Reading Rooms[5] and continue uphill to King Street.

Cross straight over and take the path half-right through a small wooded area to reach Tatton Street. Turn right past St. Vincent de Paul church and then left at the 5-way junction[4] onto Garden Road (B5083). Follow this to the A50 Manchester Road[3]. Cross with care and keep ahead down Tabley Road with The Heath on your left. In 1.4 km, at a finger post[2] just after the cemetery, take the bridleway (Swain's Walk) on the right and follow this straight ahead for 1.25 km to reach the A556 Chester Road[1]. Cross with great care, using the central refuge.

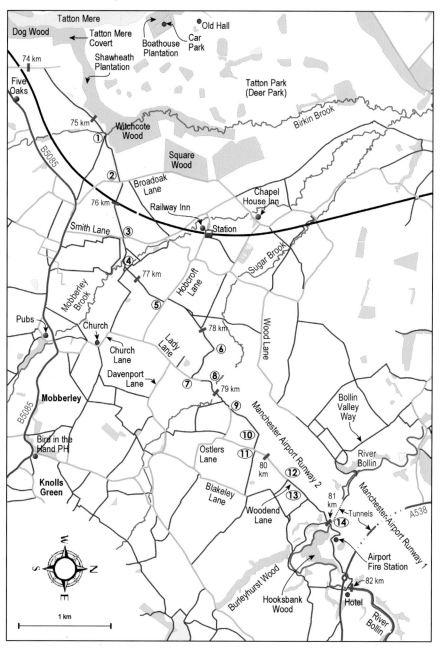

Numbers on the map refer to superscript numbers in the walking instructions

Chapter 7. Shaw Heath to the River Bollin

Shaw Heath – River Bollin (5.8 km, 3.6 mi):

Cross the footbridge[1] over Birkin Brook and climb up the field edge beside the wood, aiming for a stile beside the right-hand gate. Follow the field edge to Broadoak Lane[2]. Go over the stile almost opposite and follow the field edge to a ladder stile. Go over and cross the railway with care.

Go over another ladder stile and through a small copse; then make directly for the centre of the lowest roof on the right of the farm buildings in the distance. Exit over a stile[3] onto Smith Lane, turn right and take the first path on the left. After crossing a brook take the first stile on the left and descend a wooded bank to cross over a bridge and turn right onto a farm track. Just before the farmyard entrance, turn left[4] beside the hedge to go over a stile, cross a small paddock and another stile into a large field. Aim for the large oak and cross the nearby stile and bridge. Go straight ahead to a line of trees and then to the corner of a garden hedge. Follow the hedge to exit over a stile onto Hobcroft Lane[5].

Go left and in 60m right down a surfaced track. Continue almost to the airport fence and crash gate 10. Turn right[6] and follow the bridleway to Lady Lane[7]. Turn left, go through a gate and just before crash gate 9 turn right[8] along a bridleway beside the runway to reach Ostlers Lane near crash gate 8. Almost immediately leave the road again[9], going ahead beside the runway to a gate and footbridge[10]. Turn right onto a narrow path to reach Woodend Lane[11]. Turn left and follow the road until you reach a gate and unmade road[12]. Follow the fence on your right and soon converge with the path beside the runway fence[13]. On reaching crash gate 7, descend a steep metalled road to the footbridge[14] over the River Bollin.

River Bollin – Shaw Heath (5.8 km, 3.6 mi):

Cross the river bridge[14] and go up the road to crash gate 7. Go to the left of the crash gate and walk with the runway to the right. After passing a farm on the left, take the path bearing left[13], away from the runway. Follow the fence to a gate[12] and go through onto a surfaced track that soon becomes a road (Woodend Lane).

After 700m take the first footpath on the right[11] almost to the airport fence. Go left over a footbridge[10] and follow the right-hand fence to a finger post[9] at Ostlers Lane beside crash gate 8. Go ahead down the lane, through a gate and along a bridleway between fences. Continue to crash gate 9, go left at a finger post[8] onto Lady Lane and in 220m take the first footpath on the right[7] to crash gate 10. Go left[6] here and follow a metalled track for 750m to Hobcroft Lane. Go left and in 60m go over a stile[5] on the right. Follow the garden hedge and when it ends keep straight ahead towards a post between two oaks; then go slightly right to a stile and footbridge. Now aim for the right-hand end of the distant farm buildings, eventually crossing a stile into a paddock. Leave this by the stile opposite and walk with the hedge on your left to a farm track[4]. Go right, leave the track by the first bridge on the left and climb a wooded bank to a stile. Cross, and go right along a path beside a fence to the road (Smith Lane).

Go right on the road and almost at once left over a stile[3], then aim for the furthest point of the wooded field boundary. Cross a stile, go through a copse and over a stile to cross the railway. Cross a second stile and follow the left-hand hedge to the road (Broadoak Lane). Cross the stile[2] opposite and follow the right-hand hedge to a further stile. Follow the woodland edge on the right and descend the field to the footbridge[1] over Birkin Brook.

Tabley to the River Bollin – Cranford and Concorde

From Tabley to the River Bollin, the North Cheshire Way continues for a further 12 km across the Cheshire Plain. We are at the northern edge of the plain here, not far from the great conurbation around Manchester. The natural landscape and the underlying geology are similar to the areas we have already encountered further west and further south, but the appearance of the landscape is here much more influenced by human settlement. There are great parks and country houses - including Tatton Hall and its park, one of the grandest of them all. The ancient town of Knutsford presents a hybrid character, both market town and a growing residential centre for the wealthier commuters into the Manchester conurbation just to the north. Further east, the traditional farming landscape of the plain is again modified by the increased population of the villages that increasingly serve as dormitories for Manchester. And in an inescapable indication of modernity, and the proximity of large centres of population, the countryside hereabouts has been massively changed by the large area swallowed up by Manchester Airport (formerly "Ringway"), one of Britain's largest.

The once seemingly unchanging early Victorian orderliness of middle-class life in "Cranford" (as Mrs. Gaskell thinly disguised Knutsford in her novel) contrasts sharply with the 21st century hustle and bustle of Manchester airport, now permanent home to one of the Concorde supersonic aircraft. Ancient meets modern. One wonders what Mrs. Gaskell would have made of it all.

Tabley to Knutsford: The NCW now crosses the A556, which follows the line of Watling Street, the old Roman Road from Chester to Manchester, to leave Over Tabley along Swain's Walk, a bridleway running east through open farmland to Tabley Hill. Passing Knutsford's Tabley cemetery the route now takes the Tabley Road and enters Knutsford beside The Heath – where Betty Barker's cow fell in a lime pit (see below) – the site of a military camp in the English civil wars and of an American army camp in World War II.

Knutsford: The town is said to derive its name from the crossing of a local stream by Canute ("Knut"), king of England from 1016 to 1035 and perhaps best known to schoolboy historians for his demonstration of Christian humility by rejecting his courtiers' flattery and demonstrating that even he could not stop the tide. After fording the brook the king sat down to shake the sand from his feet, just as a wedding procession passed by. This is the claimed origin of the custom of sprinkling of red and white sand on pavements and doorsteps to celebrate a marriage – a custom still continued in the creation of coloured sand patterns on May Day.

> The lads and lassies their tun dishes hanging,
> Before all the doors for the wedding were sanding,
> I'd ask Nan to wed and she answered with ease -
> 'You may sand for my wedding as soon as you please!'
> Old Knutsford ballad

Chapter 7. Tabley to the River Bollin

The town prospered quietly in the Middle Ages as a market town and later as a coaching stop on the London road. By the 18th century, it was one of the largest settlements in Cheshire, when we find it referred to as the "Metropolis of the Eastern Hundreds". Although always primarily a residential town, a silk mill was built here in 1763 and the street still bears its name. The railway from Manchester arrived in 1862 – and still provides access to the North Cheshire Way!

The Georgian town has, of course, been preserved for us set in literary aspic by Elizabeth Cleghorn Stevenson (1810-1865), better known as the author Mrs. Gaskell. The everyday life of the ladies of Knutsford – named as "Cranford" in her eponymous novel – is remembered from her Georgian childhood living with her aunt in her "dear, adopted native town". Many of the locations in the book are still readily identified and viewed from a stroll around the town – including the site of the accident that befell Miss Barker's cow, already passed on The Heath. Mrs. Gaskell is still here, buried in the graveyard of the Brook Street Unitarian Chapel she attended as a girl. She has a street named after her – Gaskell Avenue, near The Heath – though whether she would have thought it a compliment that this is the address of "Higgins the Highwayman" is unclear. He was a character in real life, executed in 1767, who featured in her short story "The Squire's Tale". Perhaps she would prefer her memorial tower, incorporated into King's Coffee House. The Italianate tower was erected in 1907 by Richard Watt, a wealthy Manchester glove-maker and carries a bust of Mrs. Gaskell, a list of her works and another of the kings and queens of England.

Edward Higgins was far from being the only criminal to have spent "time" in Knutsford. The Sessions House, still the County Courthouse, was once part of the "House of Correction", a much larger establishment that included a gaol (demolished in the 1930s) for 800 prisoners.

Nor is the Gaskell memorial the only example of Watt's architectural taste. The Ruskin Rooms, right on the NCW and named after John Ruskin (1819-1900), Watt's favourite poet. The building combines Italianate, Moorish and Art Nouveau styles and originally served as a recreation room for workers at Watt's "Knutsford Steam Laundry" (also on the NCW, at the bottom of Drury Lane and sadly now lacking its minaret!). A little further on, just off Moorside (the road running beside the Mere) is Watt's home – again showing Islamic influences on the style – in Coronation Square. This was built to celebrate the coronation of King Edward VII in 1902.

The Ruskin Rooms

The Mere itself is a pretty spot almost in the town centre and the haunt of varied waterfowl. Occasionally rarer species can be seen – corn buntings, water rail and even a recent sighting of the elusive bittern.

Tatton Park and Hall: The NCW does not go through the park, as it is not always open, but on its way through Knutsford, it does pass the south entrance. The park and house are owned by the National Trust and managed by Cheshire County Council. Human settlement here goes back a long way: thousands of early Mesolithic flint tools have been found in the park, probably at the site of a temporary hunting camp. Some of these may be as much as 10,000 years old. Near the Old Hall there was a more permanent early Neolithic camp that has been dated to between 3500 and 2950 B.C. The oldest surviving home in the park is the Old Hall, parts of which go back to the late 1400s. The estate passed from the Tatton family in the female line to the Masseys in the 13th century and from then, again by the female line first to the Stanleys and then later to the Breretons. In Tudor times, it was sold to the Egerton family, who owned it until the line died out in 1958 when it passed to the National Trust. It was John Egerton who in 1716 completed the new house, the present Tatton Hall. In addition to the Hall, there are 50 acres of gardens, a large deer park with meres and country walks and Tatton Dale Home Farm, restored to its condition of the 1930s.

Knutsford to the River Bollin: Leaving The Mere at Knutsford, the NCW goes under the railway and climbs up to the suburb of Cross Town, before taking the Mobberley Road to the settlement of Shaw Heath, now very much part of Knutsford itself. After passing Parkgate Trading Estate, we are back into the Cheshire countryside on a path that goes across fields and

Birkin Brook

beside plantations to reach Birkin Brook, haunt of the kingfisher and the boundary between Knutsford and Mobberley. The NCW crosses the large parish of Mobberley well to the north of the village centre, taking a route across fields and past the site of the former Ilford photographic works to arrive at the south-western end of the new second runway of Manchester's international airport.

Manchester Airport: This is the country's third largest airport, home to nearly 100 airlines and handling 19 million passengers a year. The NCW runs for 3 km alongside its second runway, whose construction in 2001 proved controversial locally but also brought increased prosperity to the region. The history of aviation in Manchester began in 1910 with the first flight from London and over the years that followed there were several temporary aerodromes. The first permanent airport was opened in 1930 at Barton Moss, west of Salford. This is still used for pleasure flights, but was not a commercial success becoming too waterlogged to use after heavy rain. The present airport was constructed between 1934 and 1938 and had not long been open when World War II broke out. During the war 60,000 airborne troops were stationed there – and aircraft were manufactured at the adjacent factories of Fairey Aviation and A.V. Roe. The famous Lancaster bomber made its maiden flight from here. The airport expanded after the war and by the 1980s was an international gateway with flights to destinations worldwide. One recent visitor to the airport is here to stay – as it has become the location of G-BOAC, one of the remaining Concorde aircraft, the world's first supersonic passenger jet. Perhaps travelling through the skies at twice the speed of sound – faster than the earth spins – was not easily imagined by Ringway's first residents: a Neolithic settlement at Oversley Farm, just north of the NCW, was discovered in 1997-98 during excavations for the second runway. It survived until the Iron Age, but now lies beneath the arriving and departing aircraft.

Nearby Trails and Places to Visit

Gauntlet Birds of Prey Park: On the A50 just north of Knutsford. It has owls, falcons, vultures and eagles – and offers falconry courses!

Lower Peover: Beautiful Cheshire village with timber-framed church. Opposite the church is the pub – "Bells of Peover" – where General Patton (whose headquarters were at Peover Hall nearby) would meet General Eisenhower in 1944 while planning the Normandy landings.

Manchester Airport: Although there are splendid views of aircraft from the NCW, the official viewing area (with Concorde guided tours) is on the far side of both runways, accessible from junction 6 on the M56.

Tabley Cuckoo Clock Museum: At Nether Tabley, on the A556, 2 km south of the M6. The largest collection of Black Forest cuckoo clocks in the world that can be seen by the public. Also on display are fairground and street organs.

Tabley House: The Hall, completed in 1767 on the site of an older 14th century building, is regarded as the finest Palladian house in the north of England. It was the home of the Leicester family, and the second owner – Sir John Leicester, 1st Lord de Tabley – assembled a fine collection of paintings and furniture that remains at the hall (sometimes open to the public).

Tatton Hall: *(see above)*. The main entrance is near Rostherne, signposted from the A556.

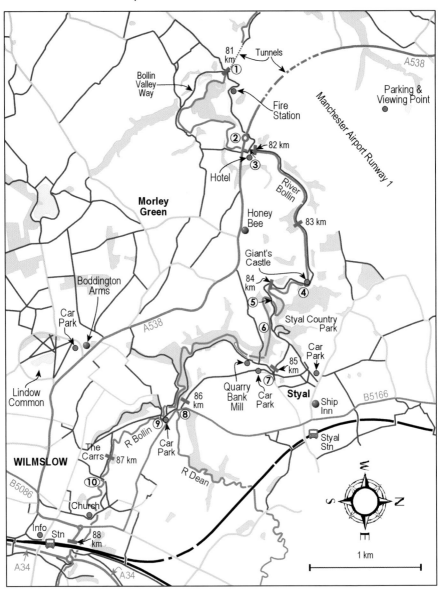

Numbers on the map refer to superscript numbers in the walking instructions

---

Cheshire Dialect

Herb Peter – a cowslip

Paigle – a primrose

River Bollin – Wilmslow (6.2 km, 3.9 mi):

Cross the bridge[1] over the River Bollin and climb up the road to crash gate 6. Take the path on the right, near the gate, follow it round the rear of the fire station and then along the embankment and down steps to the A538 roundabout[2]. Cross the main road on the side nearest the tunnel to climb up the cul-de-sac road opposite. In 50m go sharp right down the hotel service road. Just before the river bridge turn left at the map board[3] onto the path into the Styal Estate. Follow the path beside the river and in 1.6 km, after descending a long flight of steps, cross Giant's Castle Bridge[4] over the river.

Bear left away from and then back to the river, cross a level area to the far right corner, then climb and descend again to cross the river at Oxbow Bridge[5]. Go downstream with the river on your left, then take the first path on the right to cross the neck of the oxbow and reach the river again, turning left and walking upstream with the river now on your right. After 100m cross Kingfisher Bridge[6] and climb away from the river with a steep valley on the left. Take the first path right at the National Trust map board and continue to the road[7].

Turn right and almost immediately left along a path to the bus stop and the car park for Quarry Bank Mill. Go ahead along the right-hand side of the car park to a gate and finger post at the far end. Continue along the public footpath towards Wilmslow and on reaching a cycleway turn right along it. Cross the footbridge[8] over the River Dean and keep to the right of the buildings ahead. Turn right to cross the bridge[9] over the River Bollin and turn left into the park, joining the Bollin Valley Way. Follow the main path through the park ("The Carrs") parallel to the river and cross back over the river again at the second footbridge[10].

Wilmslow – River Bollin (6.2 km, 3.9 mi):

Cross the River Bollin footbridge[10] and follow the main path through the park ("The Carrs") parallel to the river. At the end of the park cross a brick bridge[9] back over the River Bollin to a car park. Bear left towards buildings and then, at a fork in the path, leave the Bollin Valley Way to go half-right and soon over a footbridge[8] over the River Dean. Continue for a short way beside the road, then go through the second gate on the left into the Styal Estate and follow the path to the Quarry Bank Mill car park. Follow the left edge of the car park and just past the bus stop descend to the road.

Go right and immediately left[7] on the path signed for Styal Woods. In 330m go left by the map board, descend to the river, turn right over Kingfisher Bridge[6] and then follow the river on your left. In 100m bear right and cross the neck of land to arrive at the river again. Go left along the bank to Oxbow Bridge[5], cross the river, turn left and soon climb up to the edge of the woods. Go along the boundary, descend steps to the river, cross a level area and follow the main path away from the river. Then follow the path back to the river at a finger post signed Oversley Ford. Cross the river by Giant's Castle Bridge[4], climb the steps on the other side and descend again to the river.

Follow the river downstream for 1.6 km until you reach the hotel service road at the map board[3]. Turn right and at the top go sharp left down to the A538 roundabout[2]. Cross the main road on the side nearest the tunnel and climb the steps on the far side. Go right at the top and follow the path along an embankment, soon passing round the rear of the fire station to reach the airport fence. Follow the fence to crash gate 6, turn left on the access road and descend to the footbridge[1] over the River Bollin.

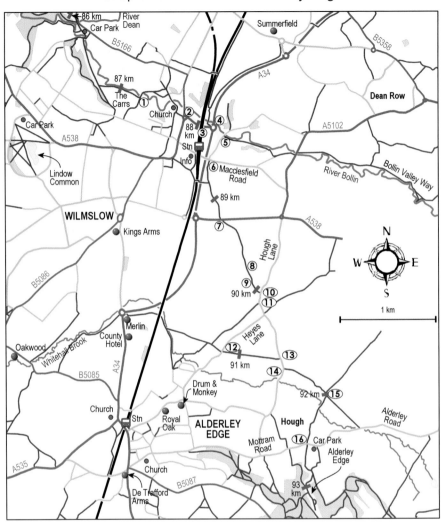

Numbers on the map refer to superscript numbers in the walking instructions

Cheshire Dialect
Demath – the amount of land that one man can mow in a day
Graft – a spade's depth

Chapter 8.   Wilmslow to Alderley Edge

Wilmslow – Alderley Edge   (5.3 km, 3.3 mi):

Continue on the Bollin Valley Way, across the river[1] and bearing right to the park exit. Leave by the stone arch, go right, passing the church to the right and sunken gardens to the left to reach the roundabout[2]. Go clockwise, crossing the Manchester Road and left under the railway[3]. Bear left on a path and soon right, under the A34[4], continuing with the river to the left to a gate[5] onto Wilmslow Park Rd. Leave the Bollin Valley Way, turning right and away from the river. On reaching the Macclesfield Rd.[6], use the crossing on the right to cross, return left and then go right on a road with a footpath sign. At the nursing home entrance take the path on its left for 360m to a turning circle. Go ahead, up steps at the far end of the road, then down steps and across the A538[7]. Go left, and in 20m right onto a path under trees and into a field. Aim for a clump of bushes, and then take the same line towards trees and – when the far field boundary comes into view - walk to the nearest corner[8]. Go left at the waymark and along the boundary to the far corner. Go over a stone bridge[9] and stile onto a path between fences. Just after entering a wood, go left along its edge and out onto Hough Lane[10]. Go right and, just after the farm, take the path right[11] into fields. Follow the boundary, go over a stile and left along a track to Heyes Lane[12]. Cross, and follow the edge of two fields to Hough Lane[13]. Go right, and then at the entrance to Brook Farm go left over a stile[14] into fields and ahead for 100m to the field edge. Follow the hedge until the path crosses it, then walk the other side of the hedge to a path junction[15]. Cross the stile and go right, along the field edge, shortly crossing a brook. Climb to a stile in the far left corner and then go along the field edge to a path between fences exiting onto Mottram Rd[16].

Alderley Edge – Wilmslow   (5.3 km, 3.3 mi):

Cross Mottram Rd.[16] and follow the path opposite between fences. Go over a stile and follow the field edge; cross another stile and keep ahead to a stile and bridge in a recessed corner. Cross the brook and follow the field edge to a corner. Go left over a stile[15] and along the hedge, in 90m crossing to the other side. Follow the hedge until it bears right, then go straight ahead to a stile. Go right on Hough Lane[14] and take the next path on the left[13]. Follow the hedge across two fields to Heyes Lane[12]; cross and take the track opposite. Go right at the first stile, follow the hedge for 600m to Hough Lane[11] and turn left. At the end of a small wood go left over a stile[10] and down a path between fences to a stile and a stone bridge[9]. Go left, cut across the recessed boundary to the hedge and go right along the hedge. Where it turns left[8], go straight up the rise to a small copse that soon comes into view. After the copse, aim slightly right to a stile in the field corner. Go over and follow the boundary to the A538[7]. Cross and go up and down steps into an estate road. At the end of this take the path ahead for 360m to emerge beside a nursing home.

Go left to the Macclesfield Rd.[6], cross using the pedestrian crossing to the left, and go down the private road ahead for 260m and then through a gate[5] on the left to join the Bollin Valley Way. Keeping the river on your right, go under the A34[4] and at the next junction go left to the road. Go right, under the railway[3] and at the roundabout[2] go anti-clockwise, crossing the Manchester Rd., and then turn right passing sunken gardens on your right and the church on your left. Cross the river, continue to the park entrance on your left, cross the car park and take the path ahead to cross the Bollin bridge[1].

River Bollin to Alderley Edge – a Cheshire Microcosm

This 11.5 km section of the NCW runs from the tunnel taking the River Bollin under the runway of Manchester airport to Hough at the foot of the sandstone scarp of Alderley Edge. Technically, we are still crossing the Cheshire Plain but this part of the route presents three completely contrasting landscapes.

For the first 4 km, as the path follows the valley of the River Bollin upstream to Styal, the river twists and turns. It has eroded through the overlying glacial clays and down into the sandstone bedrock forming a dramatic and steep-sided valley. Mudstone, siltstone and sandstone exposures show in the river bed and in the bordering rocky cliffs. Where not too steep, the slopes are clothed with ancient woodland.

Soon after leaving Styal, the picture changes from sylvan to suburban as the route passes through the town of Wilmslow and its environs. This is now a largely man-made landscape and we are reminded once more how close we in fact are to the great conurbations of Manchester and Stockport. A glance at the map shows that the middle of Stockport is only 10 km away to the north-east and Manchester City Hall only a little further to the north. Yet not all is built-up; there is the polite and well-groomed landscape of urban parkland relieving the built-up area as we remain beside the River Bollin as far as the town centre.

As the NCW turns south and leaves Wilmslow it also leaves the Bollin and soon re-enters the Cheshire Plain in its more conventional garb – a gently undulating rural landscape of farms and pastures still keeping at bay the encroaching development of Wilmslow itself and the smaller town of Alderley Edge just to the south. The latter town shares its name with the sandstone escarpment to its east and our route skirts the east of the town and ends at the small settlement of Hough at the very foot of the imposing sandstone "Edge".

The Bollin Valley from Manchester Airport to Styal: The River Bollin rises in the foothills of the Pennines and flows through Macclesfield, Wilmslow, Hale, Bowdon and Dunham Massey in its 50 km journey to the Manchester Ship canal and the River Mersey. For most of its length, it is accompanied by the Bollin Valley Way, which – like the Bollin itself passes under the

Giant's Bridge over the River Bollin

Chapter 8. River Bollin to Alderley Edge

second runway of Manchester Airport by a large tunnel that marks the beginning of this section of the NCW.

The stretch of the Bollin Valley from here to Styal runs through Styal Woods and is perhaps the prettiest section of the entire river. The woodlands are ancient and the views are enhanced by the river and the sandstone cliffs that form the steepest parts of the valley sides. Much of the valley is now owned by the National Trust. There are woodpeckers and, by the river, kingfishers flash past and dippers dart in and out of the water. The shady rocks are a rich habitat for ferns, mosses and liverworts. Woodland flowers abound, including orchids in season. The river has a variety of fish including trout and, since 2004, salmon.

Styal: As the NCW comes to the end of Styal Woods it passes Quarry Bank Mill. Like the surrounding Styal estate, this is owned by the National Trust but once belonged to the Greg family. Samuel Greg, a successful Manchester textile merchant, established the cotton mill in 1784. The position was chosen to take advantage of the fast-moving waters of the Bollin as a source of power. Although the Gregs were, by the standards of the times, enlightened employers, the story of the working conditions in the mill is a chastening reminder of the privileged lives we now lead – at least in the developed world. The mill is maintained in working condition and has the most powerful working water-wheel in Europe. The nearby Apprentice House (just off the NCW) gives an idea of the everyday life of the pauper children who constituted about one third of the work-force in the mill in the 1830s. The village of Styal, just a little further off to the north-east, was transformed from sleepy agricultural hamlet to "factory colony" by the building of the mill. The school was opened in 1823, a decade before education for factory children became compulsory. The village shop and bakery opened in the same year. Most unusually for the times, the Gregs even paid attention to sanitation (to reduce absenteeism due to ill health!) and each house in the factory community had its own back yard and outside privy.

Styal to Wilmslow: Leaving the mill, the North Cheshire Way crosses the fields of Styal Country Park – cutting across a meander of the Bollin – to emerge by the river again at the foot of Worms Hill on the way to Wilmslow. Here the Bollin is joined by its tributary, the little River Dean that descends from Lamaload Reservoir and meanders across the fields to Wilmslow. The NCW crosses both rivers and approaches

The Carrs, Wilmslow

the town of Wilmslow through The Carrs. This is a parkland area of open meadow and woodland along the course of the Bollin, forming a tamed and gentle version of the wilder Bollin valley below Styal. The valley is much wider here and the flat riverside meadows are sometimes flooded in the winter rains.

Wilmslow: With a population of 30,000, Wilmslow is the largest town encountered by the main line of the North Cheshire Way. The town has few historical connections and does not even appear in the Domesday Book. In the Middle Ages this was a rural area with a few large estates and even fewer hamlets where people eked out a living by farming, or worked for the rich landowners. There is, nevertheless, a 16th century church on the site of an older foundation and the modern town appears to have grown up as a coaching station on the road from London to Manchester. In 1894 the small settlement around St. Bartholomew's church gave its name to an amalgamation of the ancient parishes in the vicinity. It was never a major industrial centre, though at the time of the Industrial Revolution there was some button-making for the Macclesfield silk industry and at least one fustian (coarse cotton) mill. The railway came in 1842, with a second line via Styal opened up in 1909.

Wilmslow's character today seems to have little to do with Cheshire. The town and its surroundings provide homes for commuters to Manchester and Stockport and are the location of many a "des.res." owned by wealthy business-folk, "soap" stars and, of course, footballers. Several of the Manchester United team live in or around the town; Old Trafford is just 16 km away. The flavour of the town is well-conveyed by the international brand names over the luxury shops. The town accounts for one fifth of all Aston Martins sold in the UK and the local department store stocks Armani clothes and Mulberry handbags. There are boutiques and cafés, leisure clubs and hairdressers galore (one offers a fantastic "low-price" introductory offer for new clients at "only" £80 for a haircut).

A colourful former resident was "Romany" (aka the Rev. George Bramwell Evans, a Methodist minister born in Hull in 1884) whose children's nature broadcasts were a feature of "Children's Hour" on the BBC both before and after his death in 1943. For many of that generation they were an introduction to the beauties of the English countryside by a man who was the David Attenborough of his day. He retired in Wilmslow and his caravan ("vardo" in Romani) is preserved beside the library and occasionally open to visitors.

Wilmslow's most famous son may be Alan Turing, the father of computer science and pioneer of "artificial intelligence" (or, as the film has it, "AI"). He was the genius who cracked the "Enigma" codes and thus saved his country from the attempts of the U-boats to starve Britain into submission in World War II. His was one of the great minds of the 20th century but, sadly, he was driven to suicide at the age of 42 after being convicted of a consenting gay relationship. One can only wonder what more he would have achieved had he not been driven to an early grave by the intolerance of the society in which he lived.

Lindow Common with its Black Lake lies on the western edge of the town and is today a Site of Special Scientific Interest (SSSI). It is a lowland heath habitat with dragonflies, butterflies, lizards and birdlife. Nearby is the remaining 10% of Lindow Moss, a peat bog that was the grave of an anonymous, but now renowned former Wilmslow resident, "Lindow Man". He was discovered in 1984 – the leathery preserved corpse of an Iron Age man. The body is that of a 25-30 year old healthy male who died some time in the first two centuries A.D. His death was gruesome. He was beaten so that his skull and teeth were cracked, but not fatally, then garrotted and finally deposited face down in a pool of surface water. There have been other discoveries of body parts at the site, but Lindow II (as "Lindow Man" is known) is by far the most complete and is now on permanent display in the British Museum in London. The reason for his murder is uncertain, but probably represents a ritual sacrifice. One can speculate that he may have been an early British footballer who got "sent off" in a crucial match against the Romans and cost his tribe the World Cup … The ladies might also like to indulge in the "Essence of Time" range of skin care products marketed in the USA as "containing unadulterated peat from Lindow Moss" … perhaps their director of marketing has not seen the somewhat leathery condition of Lindow Man after 2000 years of treatment!

Wilmslow to Hough: The North Cheshire Way goes through the centre of Wilmslow, and then swings south away from the Bollin and out into farmland. This is the more usual Cheshire scene of farms and fields, though the urbanisation of Wilmslow and Alderley Edge (the town) is not far away. One feature on the skyline cannot be missed; the walker's eye is inexorably pulled to the impressive wooded escarpment of Alderley Edge (the ridge), drawing ever closer ahead. Some 4 km after leaving the streets of Wilmslow, we arrive at Mottram Road in the hamlet of Hough, pausing to draw breath before tackling the climb ahead.

Nearby Trails and Places to Visit

Alderley Edge: A smaller and prettier version of Wilmslow – this is another wealthy retreat with shopping for sybarites, expensive eating places and millionaires' homes tucked away down leafy lanes. There is also a railway station that serves as an alternative to Wilmslow for access to the North Cheshire Way.

Bollin Valley Way: This is a 40 km waymarked path following the Bollin Valley from Macclesfield to Partington. In the area of Styal, Wilmslow and Mottram St. Andrew it runs across, near to or with the NCW.

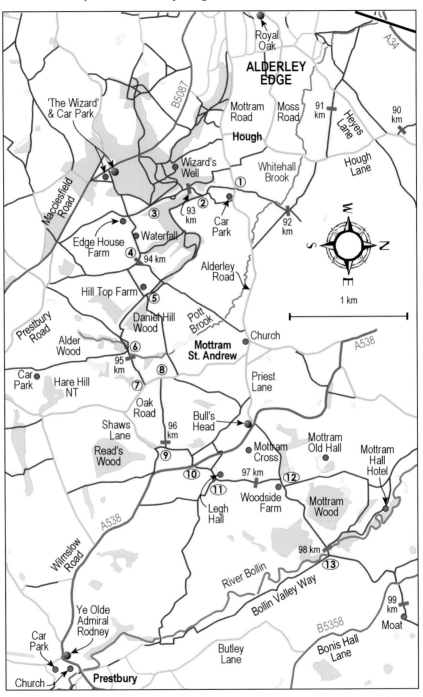

Numbers on the map refer to superscript numbers in the walking instructions

Chapter 9. Alderley Edge to Mottram St. Andrew

Alderley Edge – Mottram St. Andrew (5.5 km, 3.4 mi):

Cross Mottram Rd.[1], go up the gully, left at the fork and curve downhill to go right on another path. At the next fork[2] go uphill and right, then at a rocky outcrop go right and uphill. At the top go left onto a woodland track, then through a gate[3] and slightly left on a track to Edge House Farm. Go left through a gate, then right and at the next stile left down a track. Cross a stile[4], go between fences and at the next stile go right onto a track. Go left past converted barns. Take the track round to the left, through a gate, then sharp right[5] and uphill, over a stile and up stone steps onto the path through Daniel Hill Wood. Exit the wood, cross a stile into fields and go left along a field edge. Go right beside a fence at a post signed "Hare Hill", crossing a track and then a stile into Alder Wood. Exit by a gate[6] and go across a field, aiming for a telegraph pole, to a stile in a hollow. Go uphill, aim for the roof across the field, exit through a kissing gate and go left on Oak Rd[7].

Take the next path right over a stile[8]. Cross to a stile and follow the field edge to another stile; cross the next field, go through a gate and down to a bridge and gate[9]. Go left on a track to the A538[10]. Cross diagonally to the track to Legh Hall; where this divides, keep left to a gate[11] almost opposite the front door. Cross the field to a stile. With the hedge on the left look for a stile to cross it to the other side, then go right to the road at Woodside Farm[12]. Go right down the drive, over a stile in a tall hedge and then ahead, passing buildings on your left, to a stile. Go between a hedge and fence, then sharp left over a stile. Follow markers across the golf course to a wood; go right, through the wood and back onto the course. Go left, following waymarks, cross a stile and down to the River Bollin[13].

Mottram St. Andrew – Alderley Edge (5.5 km, 3.4 mi):

Cross the Bollin[13]; climb to a stile and follow waymarks across the golf course. Go through Mottram Wood and back to the course by the first left-hand stile. Follow the left-hand hedge briefly, then follow waymarks to a stile. Take the fenced track and cross a stile into a more open area. Pass buildings on the right, bear left and over a stile in a tall hedge then take the drive to the road. At a finger post[12] go left into the yard of Woodside Farm. Follow the left-hand hedge, after a while crossing a stile to the other side. After the next stile, continue to a stile[11] onto a track in front of Legh Hall. Go down the drive left of the house, then take a track bearing right to reach the A538[10]. Cross diagonally and go down a track for 340m. Go right at a waymark, through a gate[9] and over a bridge. Climb a rise, aiming for an electricity pole, to a gate. Cross three fields to Oak Rd[8]. Go left; opposite Turner House Farm, take the gate on the right[7].

Descend to a stile in a hollow and slightly right to a gate[6] in another hollow. Take the path (signed 'The Edge') through Alder Wood. Exit, follow a fence, go sharp right at a hedge, then ahead and over a stile on the right into Daniel Hill Wood. Exit down steps to a stile[5]. Go left and uphill, then through a gate and right on a track past converted barns; where it goes left, go right over a stile. In 120m, go left over a stile, then between fences and over a stile onto a track[4]. At the top, cross a stile by a gate, go right, cross a small field and over a stile. Go left uphill to a gate and Edge House Farm. Go right on a track; as it bends left, take a gate on the right into Dickens Wood[3]. At a clearing, go right and downhill, then over a rise to a rocky outcrop. Go down, then left and keep right to the edge of the woods[2]. Follow the woodland edge, climb the next path on the left and curve right to descend a gully to Mottram Rd[1].

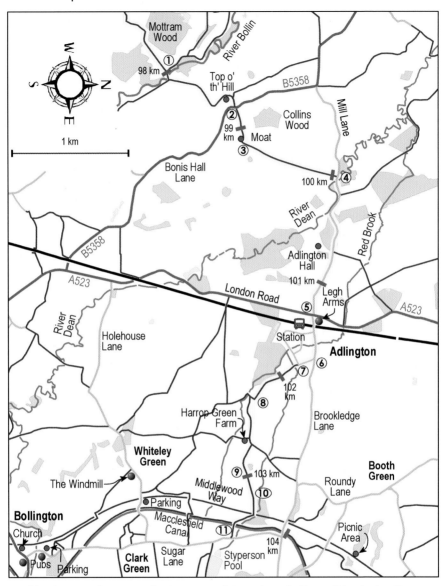

Numbers on the map refer to superscript numbers in the walking instructions

---

Cheshire Dialect

Cheshire acre = two statute acres plus one more in nine
... thus 18 Cheshire acres is 38 acres.
... and you wondered why this book mostly uses kilometres?

Chapter 9. Mottram St. Andrew to the Macclesfield Canal

Mottram St Andrew – Macclesfield Canal: (5.5 km, 3.4 mi):

Cross the River Bollin[1] and follow the finger post to the far left corner of the field. Exit and walk beside the hedge on your right to the farm (there is also a short cut straight to the farm along a permissive path). Cross the stile and go round a building to enter Top o' th' Hill Farm. Go straight ahead to a track and follow this round to the B5358 (Bonis Hall Lane)[2].

Cross the road to the stile by a field gate. Cross and follow the hedge on the right to the end of the field and then to a dry moat. Go round the moat, keeping it on your right, and through a kissing gate into a large field. Keep the fence on your right and at a finger post[3] go left. Walk to the gate at the end of the field; go through, and down the track to Mill Lane[4]. Turn right on the road and in 1.25 km carefully cross the busy A523 at the traffic lights[5]. Go past the Legh Arms, over the railway and then down the second road on the right (Wych Lane)[6].

Where the road turns right[7], keep straight ahead on a track. In 500m, where the track turns right[8], go ahead over a stile and, with the trees on the left, cross a field towards Harrop Green Farm. Pass the farm on your right and then at the first finger post turn right from the track into a field. Keep the hedge on your right to the next finger post, then bear left across the field to a stile. Cross the next field diagonally, on the same bearing, to the furthest visible left hedge corner[10]. Walk to the waymark post now visible on the crest of the hill, from where the exit stile is visible. Go over the stile and cross the Middlewood Way (disused railway) to a stile into a field. Continue with the wood on your left to reach a stile and Bridge 22[11] over the Macclesfield Canal. Do not cross the canal, but go down onto the towpath and turn left with the canal on your right.

Macclesfield Canal – Mottram St Andrew: (5.5 km, 3.4 mi):

Turn right off the towpath at Bridge 22[11] and cross a stile. With the wood on your right, descend to the Middlewood Way (disused railway). Cross to a stile by a finger post (signed Harrop Green). Go over into a field, walk to a waymark post and follow the waymarks now visible to a stile at the left corner[9] of a small wood ahead. Cross, and walk on the same bearing to a finger post in the opposite hedge. Go half-right along the hedge to a track leading to Harrop Green Farm. Go left on the track past the farm on the left. After a small wooden building on the right, go through a gate into a field. Go ahead, past a small group of trees on the right to a stile in the field corner and exit onto a track[8]. Go ahead and in 500m continue ahead[7] on Wych Lane to its T-junction with Brookledge Lane[6]. Go left, cross the railway, pass the Legh Arms and carefully cross the busy A523 at the lights[5].

Go ahead for 1.25 km along Mill Lane. After crossing the River Dean take the next track on the left[4] and then enter a large field. Aim for a waymarked electricity pole, bear left past a tree-fringed pond on the right, and aim for a finger post[3] by a fence. Bear right along the field edge; go through a gate at the top left corner and round the right-hand edge of a dry moat. Aim for the left end of the houses ahead and at the field corner keep the hedge on your left until exiting over a stile onto the B5358 (Bonis Hall Lane)[2]. Cross over, and go ahead down a track to Top o' th' Hill. Pass a path leading off to the right, walk in front of cottages and cross a stile in the right corner of the farmyard. Go left and walk beside the hedge on your left to a stile in the far corner (there is also a permissive path straight across the field). Cross, and go straight ahead to a finger post and the bridge over the Bollin[1].

Alderley Edge to the Macclesfield Canal
– Mines, Myths and Manors –

The next 11 km of the North Cheshire Way runs from the little settlement of Hough, just east of the town of Alderley Edge, to the Macclesfield Canal north of Bollington. This is the final lap across the Cheshire Plain – although the first part of the route is anything but flat! For the first 2½ km the route climbs steeply over Alderley Edge and back down into the valley of Pott Brook. The trail then runs north-eastwards over terrain that is much more undulating, and at a somewhat higher altitude, than most of the Cheshire Plain. It circles for 3 km south and then east of the village of Mottram St. Andrew before making its third and final crossing of the River Bollin. For the next couple of kilometres it climbs over slightly higher ground and descends again to the River Dean, the small tributary of the Bollin whose confluence we passed on our way into Wilmslow. Leaving the Dean the route continues past Adlington Hall and in a couple of kilometres reaches the village of the same name. The last part of this section begins the climb out of the Cheshire Plain, ascending to the level of the Macclesfield Canal that forms an approximate boundary between the Cheshire Plain to the west and the south-west Peak District to the east.

This is a varied rural landscape. The Edge is a reminder of the central Cheshire sandstone ridge we crossed between Alvanley and Frodsham and is for the most part well-wooded. The rest of the route is through farmland and parkland, with the influence of the nearby cities of Stockport and Manchester to be seen in the addition of horticulture and market gardening to the usual mix of arable and dairy farming. The built environment also displays a mixture of traditional Cheshire farmhouses and cottages (many now renovated and developed as homes for well-heeled commuters) with larger halls in their own parks, some still privately owned, others now used as hotels. Careful planning has limited the amount of new housing in and around the villages – so market forces have escalated prices with some villages, especially Prestbury just to the south, very much the Manchester "stockbroker belt" with "celebrities" among the local residents.

Throughout much of the walk there are views eastwards to the higher hills of the Peak District … a first sign that we are nearing the end of both Cheshire and the North Cheshire Way.

Alderley Edge: The 200 metre high, 3 kilometre long ridge crossed by the NCW gives its name to the small town just to the west. "The Edge" is a wooded sandstone escarpment that owes its existence to a series of geological faults that have thrust the pebbly Helsby Sandstone more than 100 metres above the surrounding plain. The rocks are rich in metals – copper, cobalt, lead and zinc – that were mined for many years leaving some 12 km of underground tunnels. Above ground, this is a popular area for walkers and nature lovers with a network of paths through the woods and excellent views across the Cheshire Plain, to the Pennine hills to the east and to the great cities of Manchester and Stockport to the north. There is even a waterfall – almost on the NCW at the head of Waterfall Wood. The woodlands are predominantly of mature oak and beech. Similar trees, together with planted pines, are an attractive feature of the shady lanes of the town. Beneath the trees are typical woodland flowers in their season – bluebells and wild garlic, primroses and wood anemones. The bird life is quite rich and local species include green woodpeckers, little owls, redpolls, tree pipits and tree creepers.

Copper Mines

Alderley Edge was inhabited as early as the Neolithic period (the "New Stone Age"), some 5000 years ago, and evidence has been found of fire-making at Castle Rock as well as worked flints and other evidence of settlement. The Armada Beacon, erected in 1578 and used ten years later to warn of the approaching Spanish Armada, also stands on a mound capped by a stone plinth that marks the site of a Bronze Age barrow (tomb). It was in the Bronze Age, too, that the copper mining began and the site is the best preserved of its kind in Britain. The attraction of the location to these early miners was undoubtedly that the veins of ore were exposed and traces of green malachite ore can still be found on the surface. Many of the mines lay south of the ridge at Brynlow, but nearer to the NCW, south-west of Dickens Wood, is the Engine Vein, which is of similar antiquity. There are other earthworks in the area – notably in Dickens Wood –some of which may be more recent in origin.

Very close to the NCW as it runs beside Dickens Wood is the "Golden Stone". It is of Bronze Age provenance and is likely to have been an early "waymark" on the trackway to the mines and was probably later used as a boundary marker. The one impostor here is the "Druid's Circle" between Stormy Point and the Armada Beacon. Despite its evocative name this stone circle is a relatively recent "folly" and its pseudonym of the "Hanoverian Circle" is more accurate. It is about 200 years old and was probably constructed by the local stonemason Robert Garner (see below).

The mines were abandoned in early Roman times but mining began again in the modern era towards the end of the 17th century and continued intermittently until 1919 yielding many thousands of tons of copper. The principal workings –

Engine Vein, West Mine and Wood Mine – were sealed off in the 1940s after a number of accidents to amateur "explorers". However, guided tours are occasionally available courtesy of the Derbyshire Caving Club.

"The Edge" is also rich in legend, with a resurgence of interest occasioned by the Cheshire author Alan Garner. He still lives locally and is the great-great-grandson of the local stonemason Robert Garner, the creator of the Druid's Circle and the carvings at the Wizard's Well. Although often regarded as a children's writer, his works are decidedly for "children of all ages" and his first novel "The Weirdstone of Brisingamen" was widely acclaimed as were several later works, including "The Owl Service" and "The Stone Book Quartet".

The *Weirdstone* is based around the local legend of a wizard (perhaps Merlin?), the guardian of a great cavern below The Edge where rest the 'Sleepers', a company of knights – some say led by King Arthur – asleep and awaiting the call to arms to aid England in her hour of greatest need. The whole area is rich in this and other legends of probable Celtic origin. Among other unusual visitors to and residents on The Edge are a misogynist hermit, who lived in the quarry in the early 20th century to avoid the ladies, and a witches' coven (perhaps ladies to be avoided?) that was broken up in the 1960s – or perhaps just went underground, literally or otherwise.

The Wizard

Yet some men say in many parts of England that King Arthur is not dead … and men say that he shall come again … there is written upon his tomb this verse:

Hic jacet Arthurus, Rex quondam, Rexque futurus

Here lies Arthur – Once and Future King

Le Morte D'Arthur, Sir Thomas Malory

The wizard can still be seen today at his well below the lip of the Edge, with Robert Garner's carving of the wizard and the inscription: *"Drink of this and take thy fill for the water falls by the Wizhard's will"*.

Alderley Edge to the River Bollin: The NCW climbs down from The Edge through Daniel Hill Wood into the parish of Mottram St. Andrew and, crossing Pott Brook, passes to the south of the village itself. Here too were copper mines (Granger's Shaft), though now flooded and inaccessible, and Bronze Age axes have been found. The locality has given its name to the mineral "mottramite" – a colourful ore of lead and vanadium that was first discovered in the mine in the 19th century. East of the village, the NCW crosses the golf course of Mottram Hall (1753), now a hotel in mature parkland laid out in the mid-18th century with a lake and woodland. The Old Hall, south-west of the hotel stands on the site of a mediaeval moated manor house. After Mottram Wood, the path reaches the River Bollin for the third and final time – here flowing through peaceful parkland very different both from the formal parks in Wilmslow and from the wild clough woodland downstream of Styal.

River Bollin to Adlington: Crossing the Bollin, the NCW climbs over the shoulder of land between this river and its tributary the little River Dean, which is reached at Mill Lane. The Dean rises below Shining Tor in the hills to the east and flows via Lamaload Reservoir through Rainow and Bollington, to join the Bollin between Wilmslow and Styal.

Adlington: After crossing the Dean we arrive in Adlington, passing the main gate to Adlington Hall. The house has been home to the Legh family since the early 14th century and is built on the site of a Saxon hunting lodge. The east end of the Great Hall is supported by two great oaks, part of the original building constructed between 1480 and 1505. Between the trees stands the 17th century organ at whose keyboard Handel is said to have composed *The Harmonious Blacksmith* after visiting the village smithy. The Hall is a manor house standing around a quadrangle and was formerly surrounded by a moat. Much of the house was built in Tudor times in "black and white" Cheshire timbered style. The Palladian south front and west wing were added in the mid-18th century. At which time the gardens, through which runs the River Dean, were landscaped in the style of Capability Brown. The village stands on the east side of the main London road. The Macclesfield branch of the Manchester and Birmingham railway came here in 1845 and brought increased prosperity to the local farms that could more readily ship their milk to the burgeoning population of the cities to the north. There was also small-scale coal mining in the 18th century, with the Macclesfield Canal being used for transportation.

Adlington to the Macclesfield Canal: The NCW leaves Adlington beside Wych Wood to begin its 50 metre climb to the level of the Macclesfield Canal. This is a foretaste of things to come, as the canal marks the eastern limit of the Cheshire Plain. Ahead lie the Peak District hills ... and the final stage of Cheshire's longest footpath.

Nearby Trails and Places to Visit

Hare Hill: Woodland and walled gardens; colourful displays of rhododendrons and azaleas, as well as an outstanding collection of hollies. Walks in the surrounding parkland and a link path to the North Cheshire Way. National Trust.

Nether Alderley: 15th century corn mill (National Trust), 14th century church, and old cottages.

Prestbury: Saxon cross, Norman church in the grounds of the parish church; the main street has old coaching inns and many black-and-white buildings.

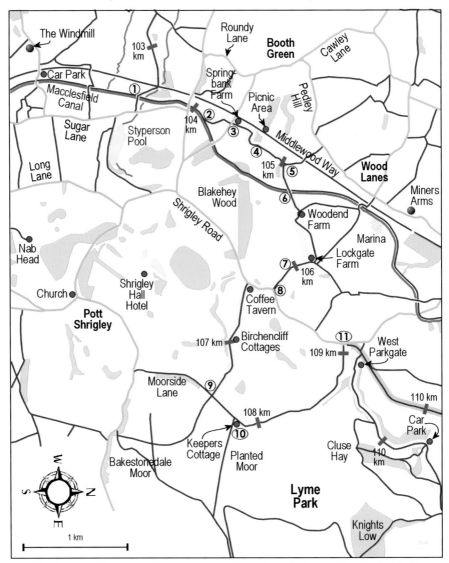

Numbers on the map refer to superscript numbers in the walking instructions

The main line of the North Cheshire Way goes through Lyme Park. This is owned and managed by the National Trust and partly financed by Stockport Metropolitan Borough Council. The Park is normally open during daylight hours, but is typically closed before 8.00 a.m. and after 8.30 p.m. (April to mid-October) or after 6.00 p.m. (mid-October to March). A more westerly alternative route is available, shown in pink on the map above and, like the rest of the North Cheshire Way, is always open.

Chapter 10. Macclesfield Canal to Lyme Park

Macclesfield Canal – Lyme Park: (5.6 km, 3.5 mi):

Go left[1] along the towpath with the canal on your right. After going under the next bridge take the next path on the left[2]. Go to the right of small trees around a pond and then left to the field corner ahead. Cross a stile and follow the right-hand fence to the road. Dogleg left and right across the road[3] to take the drive almost opposite towards Springbank Farm. Leave this track where it turns sharp right and take a path on the right past buildings and then across mown grass in front of a house, leaving the area by a stile. Follow the path round to the left, cross a bridge[4] and climb up beside a wood. Bear right at the top and aim for a house, following waymark posts. Pass the left corner of a garden and then aim for a stile onto a track. Go left on the track, keep right when it forks[5] and cross the canal bridge[6]. Go past a caravan site to the entrance to Woodend Farm. Take the permissive path to the right through a squeeze stile to go around the farm. Go over a stile beside a finger post and cross the field in the direction indicated to exit to the right of the farm ahead. Cross into the next field and aim half-right to the field edge[7], then go left along the field edge, exit onto a track and follow it to Shrigley Road[8].

Cross the road, turn right and after passing the *Coffee Tavern* restaurant take the bridleway on the left. 500m after Birchencliff Cottages, go left at a finger post[9] onto Moorside Lane. Keep straight ahead, pass Keepers Cottage and in 110m go left over a wall stile[10]. Follow the path downhill and across a stream, then beside a wall and down a steep bank to a pair of gates. Continue on the main track to Shrigley Road. Go right on the road, pass the chapel on your right and at once go sharp right[11] to enter Lyme Park. (*If the park is closed: as the road bears left, keep straight ahead onto a footpath – see next section*).

Lyme Park – Macclesfield Canal: (5.6 km, 3.5 mi):

Exit Lyme Park, go left[11] on Shrigley Road, pass a chapel on the left and then go left again up a gravel road towards cottages and a farm (*this is also the turning if approaching from the alternative route that avoids Lyme Park*). In 100m bear right and continue on the main track. Go through a pair of gates, up a steep bank, beside a wall and across a stream. Climb a steep bank and continue to a wall stile[10]. Go right onto Moorside Lane and straight on past Keepers Cottage to a finger post[9] at a path crossing. Go right and descend past Birchencliff Cottages to Shrigley Road.

Go right past the *Coffee Tavern* and, in 220m where the road bends right, go left[8] on a track to a gate into fields. Follow the left-hand hedge for half the length of the field, and then go half-right[7] across the field to a finger post and stile to the left of Lockgate Farm. At the finger post go half-left towards Woodend Farm, aiming for a pylon beyond some trees. Cross a stile on the far side of the field and take the narrow permissive path around the farm. Go left on the track, pass a caravan site and go over the canal bridge[6]. Go left at a junction[5] where the track turns sharp right. Before the next house take the path on the right, go over a stile, turn left and follow waymark posts towards a wood. Continue down to a stile and bridge[4] at the corner of the field, cross and keep the wood on the right to a stile at the top of a rise. Go over, pass the house on the right, cross a mown grass area, go past buildings and cross a stile onto a drive. Go left and, on reaching the road[3], dogleg left and right to cross a stile with a finger post signed 'Canal'. Follow the fence and cross a stile into a large field. Aim to the left of trees round a pond and bear right to a stile hidden in the far hedge. Cross onto the canal towpath[2], go right and continue to Bridge 22[1].

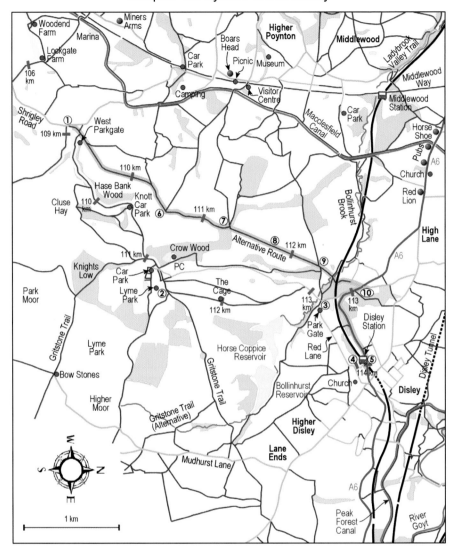

Numbers on the map refer to superscript numbers in the walking instructions

The main line of the North Cheshire Way goes through Lyme Park. This is owned and managed by the National Trust and partly financed by Stockport Metropolitan Borough Council. The Park is normally open during daylight hours, but is typically closed before 8.00 a.m. and after 8.30 p.m. (April to mid-October) or after 6.00 p.m. (mid-October to March). A more westerly alternative route is available, shown in pink on the map above and, like the rest of the North Cheshire Way, is always open.

Chapter 10. Lyme Park to Disley

Lyme Park – Disley Station: (5.0 km, 3.1 mi):

Turn sharp right off Shrigley Road[1] and enter Lyme Park. Follow the track round to the left through a wooded valley to Knott Car Park and then follow the road to Lyme Park house. Keep going in roughly the same direction, leaving the main car park and the information booth on your right, and follow the path to the house. At the entrance gates to the house, turn left[2] and walk up a broad mown grass path aiming directly for the folly ("The Cage") on the hilltop. Descend the ridge to the main park entrance kiosk[3] and turn right here to leave the park by the side gate onto Red Lane. After 700m the road bends sharp left and steeply downhill for 60m and then it turns sharp right. At this second bend leave the road[4], going straight ahead through a gate and down a flight of steps to Disley Station[5] and the end of the North Cheshire Way.

Alternative Route: *A more westerly alternative route is available for this section and may be used if Lyme Park is closed. Instead of entering the park, where Shrigley Road[1] bears left bear right (on the first footpath after the chapel). Keep ahead up the side of the hill, ignoring a track to your left, and after about 1 km, when the hillside on your right retreats to allow a view down into the valley, bear slightly right and descend to cross a small valley and. As the path begins to rise again, keep slightly left at the crossing of paths[6]. In 720m keep ahead and slightly right at a further path crossing[7], aiming for the highest point[8] of the ridge ahead. Keep on the same bearing and descend to the railway line. Cross, and follow the signed path to join Coppice Lane. Go ahead to the main A6 (Buxton Road West)[10]. Turn right and follow the main road to Disley Station[5], which is on the right after about 1 km.*

Pedestrian entry to Lyme Park is free. Charges apply for parking and for visits to the house or gardens.

Disley Station to Lyme Park: (5.0 km, 3.1 mi):

Leave the south (Stockport/Manchester) side of Disley Station[5] by walking away from the station and up the flight of steps opposite to a gate onto Red Lane[4]. Keep straight ahead and uphill for 60m then follow the road sharp right, ignoring signs for the Gritstone Trail. After 700m enter the side entrance to Lyme Park through gates and go ahead to the pay kiosk[3] on the main entrance road. Go left along the road and in 210m bear left on the track that follows the line of the ridge up to the folly ("The Cage") on the hilltop. From here descend by the broad mown strip of grassland, aiming towards the main house. On reaching the entrance gates to the house, go right[2] on a major track (the Gritstone Trail) to arrive at the main car park. Keep straight ahead, leaving the information booth and the car park on your left. Go over a cattle grid onto the road signed for the Knott car park. Pass the car park entrance and continue on a wide track through Hase Bank Wood to the park exit and turn left onto the Shrigley Road[1].

Alternative Route: *A more westerly alternative route is available for this section and may be used if Lyme Park is closed. Leave Disley Station[5] on the north (Buxton) side and go left for 1 km on the A6 main road (Buxton Road West). Pass the entrance to Lyme Park and in 200m go left[10] down Coppice Lane. Where this turns right, keep straight ahead and follow the path across the railway and over a brook to reach a path crossing[9] at Elmerhurst Cottage. Keep straight ahead, ascend the line of the ridge to the summit[8], then descend on the same bearing to a path crossing[7] beside Platt Wood. Go straight ahead with the woods on your left, then traverse uphill to a further path crossing[6]. Bear slightly right across a small valley, curve around the hillside below the ridge on your left, then descend to a stream and then briefly uphill onto the Shrigley Road[1]and turn left past the chapel.*

Macclesfield Canal to Disley – into the hills

The last 11 km of the North Cheshire Way crosses very different terrain from the rest of the route. After a deceptively gentle beginning along the towpath of the Macclesfield Canal, there is a brief excursion back towards the Cheshire Plain as if the path were reluctant to leave this familiar landscape. But soon the path plucks up courage, swings back over the canal and climbs up into the hills.

This is a very different Cheshire. The land climbs as we enter the Peak District and the views expand. This is gritstone country, older and harsher than the Triassic sandstones of the Cheshire plain. The millstone grit and its associated shales were laid down 320 million years ago in the Carboniferous period. Then the Peak District was a delta where a great river flowed into the ocean, alternately depositing sand and mud as the river channels shifted. Over millennia, the interleaved sediments were compressed; the sand turned to Millstone Grit and the mud to shale. Rivers sculpted the land into its present forms, with the slopes deeply cut by fast-flowing streams and rivers while the higher land forms rolling moors. Beneath the upland core there are lower rounded hills falling to narrow valleys and subsiding towards the undulating eastern Cheshire Plain.

Farms and barns are robust, low-built of gritstone and looking a little grim as they shelter from the wind. The hedges of the lower land are progressively replaced by dry gritstone walls. Dairy farming is accompanied by the rearing of beef cattle, some sheep – and grouse shooting on the moors. The foothills have grassland, some "unimproved" and forming flower-rich hay meadows with low scrub, tussocky grass and rushes in the valley bottoms. There is broad-leaved woodland in the valleys while small groups of trees shelter isolated farmhouses and bracken clings to the valley sides. The higher ground is moorland – rocky, with

Orchid in a meadow on the NCW

wet flushes and gullies for the many small streams. This is a landscape of heather and gorse, grasses and rushes. Looking back west on a clear day the view encompasses all of the Cheshire Plain with the Welsh mountains a blue smudge in the distance. A keen eye, aided by a little imagination, could trace the whole course of the North Cheshire Way from Wirral and Chester, across the plain, over the sandstone ridge, up the Weaver valley, and across the lowlands to the scarp of Alderley Edge before reaching the steep slopes beneath our feet.

The route leaves the higher land to enter Lyme Park and ends as the Peak District gives way to the "Manchester Pennine Fringe", making a quite sharp transition from open moors to densely populated urban areas. The North Cheshire Way ends at Disley Station, whose two platforms mark the contrast. An "up" train will reach the centre of Manchester in half an hour: a "down" train to Buxton will have you in the Peak District hills in just thirty minutes.

Chapter 10. Macclesfield Canal to Disley

Macclesfield Canal: The first 600m of this part of the NCW runs along the towpath of the Macclesfield Canal. This was built under the supervision of Thomas Telford, to link the Peak Forest Canal to the north and the Trent & Mersey Canal to the south. It opened in 1831, one of the last narrow canals to be built, and was a major artery for the products of the local coalmines and stone quarries and the silk industry of Macclesfield. It is one of the

Macclesfield Canal

highest canals in the country, running at the summit level of the Marple flight of locks on the Peak Forest Canal, more than 50m above the Cheshire Plain. There are no locks until the Dane Valley south of Macclesfield. Many of the bridges are built from the local gritstone, much of which came from the former quarries at Styperson Park, just across the canal. The canal eventually lost out to competition from the parallel railway that opened in 1869. Ironically, this closed in 1970 (and is now the Middlewood Way – see below), while the canal took on a new lease of life as a leisure waterway.

Macclesfield Canal to Pott Shrigley: This land – including Lyme Park itself – once formed part of the great royal Forest of Macclesfield created by William I in 1086. Over the years the actual "forest" (a term designating a royal hunt, not necessarily woodland) dwindled and today the deer are only in Lyme Park itself. The NCW leaves the canal just before the site of the former wharf at

Gritstone Country

Ryles Wood and descends into Jepson Clough before climbing back and crossing the canal. The climb continues and the gradients steepen as the path climbs up and away from the canal. After crossing the Shrigley Road, the route becomes steeper still and the climb up past Birchencliff to Keepers Cottage brings the walker to the highest point of the whole route – just beyond Keepers Cottage at 287m (941 feet) above sea level. Man was here millennia ago and there are prehistoric remains in this high country – at Nab Head to the south and at Reed Hill and Sponds Hill to the east, but none very close to the NCW. The present day village of Pott Shrigley centres around St. Christopher's church and Shrigley Hall, both lying south of the route. Notorious as the home of the 15-year old heiress, Ellen Turner, victim of an early 19th century deception, abduction and forced marriage ("the Shrigley Abduction"), the Hall is now a luxury hotel.

Lyme Park: From the high moors, the NCW descends steeply to the Pott Shrigley boundary. It enters Lyme Park by the western gate, climbs up the valley through Hase Bank Wood to the car park below the hill known as the Knott and then descends gently to Lyme Park house itself.

Lyme Park and Mr. Darcy's Lake

The park is the easternmost of Cheshire's great estates. It was enclosed from the royal forest in 1388 by Piers Legh and the family continued to live there for almost 600 years until the rigours of World War II made it impossible to maintain the estate and it was given to the National Trust. The hall was originally just a hunting lodge surrounded by a deer park. The present hall is of Tudor origin, made over in Palladian style in the 18th century. There is fine furniture, some notable Grinling Gibbons wood carvings and a large collection of clocks. The house's most recent fame stems from its role as "Pemberley", Mr. Darcy's country estate, in the BBC television adaptation of Jane Austen's *Pride and Prejudice*. The gardens are extensive and beautiful – with Mr. Darcy's lake, an orangery and, in counterpoint, a semi-wild woodland garden ascending a clough to the moorland edge. All is surrounded by the deer park that climbs up almost to the top of the moors at Sponds Hill. There are still herds of red and fallow deer. The furthest bounds of the park are marked by the Bowstones. These shafts of two Saxon crosses were partially destroyed in Puritan times, and probably re-erected in the 16th century as boundary markers. Lower down, lost in the undergrowth of Knightslow Wood, there are Bronze Age barrows.

After the house, the NCW climbs up to the Cage – a 16th century stone tower on its eponymous hill. It seems to have served first as a hunting lodge, then as a prison for poachers and eventually as a home for the Park Keeper. As you toil up the hill, recall that his drinking water came from a well at the bottom of it!

The Cage

Disley: The North Cheshire Way leaves Lyme Park by a side gate onto Red Lane and follows this leafy road past large secluded houses before making a final steep descent down steps to the yard of Disley Station. The village stands above the valley of the River Goyt. It benefited from its proximity to Lyme Park and grew as a staging post on the London turnpike. In the 18th century the Peak Forest Canal arrived, bringing limestone from the White Peak to Manchester. Rapid growth followed in the 19th century with the building of cotton mills, with candlewick a local speciality. The railway came in 1857 and still provides transport back into the city. Close to the NCW there is the 16th century parish church with good Continental stained glass. And for the thirsty walker, there are too many pubs to record on the map.

The ridge walk, by-passing Lyme Park: As indicated on the mapping pages, Lyme Park is not always open and therefore a more westerly alternative route from the west gate of Lyme Park to Disley station has been provided and waymarked. The combination of this with the main line makes a pleasant circular walk of about 10 km (6 miles) from Disley station.

The alternative route leaves the valley at the west gate of Lyme Park, traverses the hillside the far side of Hase Bank Wood from the main route and climbs steadily to peak at 240m on a shoulder of Hase Bank. There are excellent views west over the plain and to the higher Peak District hills peeping over the eastern ridge. Some 3 km beyond leaving the west park gate, the route starts its descent into the valley of Bollinhurst Brook, crosses the railway and emerges onto the A6 Buxton Road for a final 1 km lap of road walking to Disley Station.

Nearby Trails and Places to Visit

Cheshire Ring Canal Walk: Longer than the North Cheshire Way but not entirely in Cheshire, this runs for 155 km along six canals. It shares the towpath with the North Cheshire Way's Macclesfield Canal section.

Gritstone Trail: A beautiful hilly ridge walk of 55 km from Disley to Kidsgrove. Shares its northern end with the NCW and crosses it again in Lyme Park.

Higher Poynton: There is a visitor centre close to the canal. The Anson Museum tells the history of the Anson colliery and of the internal combustion engine.

Ladybrook Valley Trail: A 15 km valley walk from Bollinhurst Reservoir and Lyme Park to Abney Hall by the River Mersey in Cheadle, south of Manchester. Crosses the NCW near the main entrance to Lyme Park.

Middlewood Way: Cycleway and footpath running for 18 km from Marple to Macclesfield, along the former railway line parallel to the Macclesfield Canal. Crosses the NCW just west of the canal.

Peak District hills seen from the North Cheshire Way. The end ... well, almost ... for Derbyshire, just the beginning!

USEFUL INFORMATION
Transport

Although public transport is somewhat sparse and infrequent outside the major conurbations, we encourage walkers to use it where possible and to minimise the use of private cars. Where car use cannot be avoided, do consider sharing – ideal for linear walks on a section of the path.

Buses: The best source for current information on bus services is the County Council web site at: www.cheshire.gov.uk/transport/PTI/pubtraninfo.htm. This gives useful town and county maps of bus services, a summary listing of services, a link to timetables and a journey planner. Alternatively, telephone Cheshire Traveline – currently on (0870) 608-2608 – but be aware that calls to this number are charged at higher than normal rates. Current timetables and information should also be available on request by sending an e-mail to traveline@cheshire.gov.uk. The following towns and villages on the North Cheshire Way, listed from west to east, have scheduled bus services at the time of writing.

Hooton	Helsby	Styal
Backford	Frodsham	Wilmslow
Backford	Acton Bridge	Adlington
Stoak	Barnton	Lyme Park
Bridge Trafford	Anderton	Disley
Little Barrow	Great Budworth	*... and on the spur route*
Dunham-on-the-Hill	Tabley	Chester
Alvanley	Knutsford	

Car: The maps in this book show a selection of car parks on or near the route. Some of these are free, but many of them require payment (make sure you take change for pay-and-display machines). It is often possible to find roadside parking for one or two cars, either in a lay-by or on the verge. In most cases, the roadside verge forms part of the public highway and may be used for parking so long as it does not cause an obstruction. Do be sensitive to others – don't park where you would feel uncomfortable if it were *your* house nearby and be aware of the needs of farmers and others for access to their property or their land. If you act as a guest in the countryside, the countryside will make you welcome!

Trains: The best sources for current information on train services are the National Rail web site at www.nationalrail.co.uk and the TrainLine web site at www.thetrainline.com. Both sites include a journey planner that seems to work well even for the minor village stations around Cheshire.

The following railway stations, listed from west to east, are on or near the North Cheshire Way.

Hooton	Styal (¾ km NE)
Capenhurst (1 km NE)	Wilmslow (¼ km NW)
Helsby (1 km NW)	Alderley Edge (1½ km SW)
Frodsham (1 km N)	Adlington
Acton Bridge (1½ km S)	Disley
Hartford (3 km S)	*... and on the spur route*
Northwich (2 km SE)	Bache (1 km NE)
Knutsford (½ km NW)	Chester
Mobberley (1 km N)	

Refreshment

The towns along the route have a variety of places of refreshment – restaurants, tea rooms and cafés and – of course – pubs. In the countryside and the country villages the best chance of a drink or a snack – is the local pub. Some are open all day, although opening hours do vary widely and, except at weekends, many pubs are still closed from about 3.00 pm to about 6.00 pm. No attempt has been made to list specific establishments as phone numbers, proprietors and landlords all change. However, the maps in each chapter show most of the pubs on or near the route in country areas but for reasons of space, no attempt has been made to list pubs in the larger centres of population. Please note that the authors have not yet had the chance to test all of the pubs mentioned – so the inclusion or exclusion of any particular hostelry is neither a recommendation nor a warning.

Further information – particularly on pubs, but also on other places of refreshment, may be found on web sites such as:

http://www.beerintheevening.com/pubs/search.shtml

http://www.pub-explorer.com/index.html

http://www.allpubs.co.uk/

http://www.192.com/directory.cfm

http://www.pubinnguide.com/pubsidx6x0x2x.asp

http://www.oldeworldepubs.co.uk/

http://www.information-britain.co.uk/typestowns.cfm?county=33

http://myweb.tiscali.co.uk/hardpeg/pubs/cheshire%20pubs.htm

http://www.pubsgalore.co.uk/counties/cheshire/

Accommodation

Cheshire is well provided with places to stay – from luxury hotels (that may not welcome muddy boots!) to friendly bed-and-breakfasts. Again, we have not attempted to list any particular establishments as circumstances change too often. For many people the internet will provide the most convenient resource for locating accommodation convenient for walking the North Cheshire Way. The following web sites may be useful:

http://www.information-britain.co.uk/counties.cfm?county=33

http://www.bedandbreakfast-directory.co.uk/results.asp?county=Cheshire

http://www.theuktourist.com/england/chesh.html

http://www.hotelsandguesthouses.net/accommodation-Cheshire-5-1.htm

http://www.bedandbreakfasts-uk.co.uk/northwestframe.htm

http://www.guestaccom.co.uk/cheshire.htm

http://www.know-britain.com/hotels_guest_houses/cheshire.html

http://www.bedandbreakfast.com/cheshire.html

http://www.bedandbreakfasts.co.uk/propertysearch.asp?county=Cheshire

Navigation

As has been mentioned in the section on "How to walk the Path", the NCW is well waymarked and it should be possible to walk the route using only this book and the waymarks along the way. Key points in the walking instructions are linked to key numbers on the maps by superscript numerals. However, we do strongly recommend that walkers should also be equipped with a suitable Ordnance Survey map. The best maps for walkers are those in the "Explorer" series) at a scale of 1:25000 (i.e. 1 cm on the map represents 250 m on the ground, or about 2½ inches to the mile). Maps 266 (Wirral & Chester), 267 (Northwich & Delamere Forest) and 268 (Wilmslow, Macclesfield & Congleton) cover almost the entire route, with the eastern extremity just falling onto Map OL1 (Dark Peak). A less useful alternative is to use the motoring maps from the "Landranger" series at a scale of 1:50000 (1 cm on the map represents 500 m on the ground, or about 1 inch to the mile). Maps 117 (Chester & Wrexham), 118 (Stoke-on-Trent & Macclesfield) and 109 (Manchester, Bolton & Warrington) cover the route, but unfortunately its eastern half switches back and forth along the edges of the latter two maps (which do not overlap).

National Grid References: We have chosen not to use grid references in this book. They are, however, so useful and so widely used in walkers' guides and on web sites that we felt a brief word was appropriate here. In particular, if you want to report problems or errors, providing a grid reference for the location will make it much easier to deal with the issue.

Many people think that grid references are "difficult" or "mysterious". They are not! A grid reference is just describes a location in numbers, without using words. It does this by telling how far east and how far north you have to go from a fixed reference point. The distance east is called the "easting". The distance north is called the "northing". The distances are measured in metres, but these are usually approximated to the nearest 100 metres. To keep the numbers short, the country is divided into 100 x 100 km squares (hectads), each with a two-letter name. Within any hectad, a location (to within 100 metres) can be specified by a six figure number that gives the easting and the northing from the south-west corner of the square. For the area of the NCW all locations fall within the square labelled "SJ" – so it is not necessary to repeat this every time.

Thus, a grid reference of 123 456 means that the spot lies 12300 metres (12.3 km) east and 45600 metres (45.6 km) north of the southwest corner of the "SJ" square. All Ordnance Survey maps show the national grid as a series of 1 km x 1 km squares, with the easting and northing numbers along the edges of the map at 1 km (1000 m) intervals. So it is easy to give a six-figure grid reference by using these numbers and estimating by eye the number of "tenths of a square". It really is easier (and far more precise) than saying "in the middle of the wood that is a bit downhill from the second farm down the road from the village"!

A picture tells a thousand words, so here's an example:

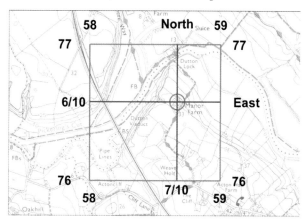

Look at Manor Farm near the middle of the map. It has an easting between 58 and 59 and a northing between 76 and 77. Estimating by eye, the farm is about seven tenths of the way from 58 to 59, so the more precise easting is 587. Similarly, it is about six tenths of the way from 76 to 77, so the more precise northing is 766. As this is near the NCW it is in the hectad square "SJ" – so the full six-figure grid reference is **SJ 587 766**. This gives the position of Manor Farm to within 100 metres – good enough for most purposes – including being rescued by the emergency services if the worst comes to the worst!

The Mid-Cheshire Footpath Society

The North Cheshire Way was created by The Mid-Cheshire Footpath Society, who have also written and published this guide. The Society is a registered charity that has been caring for mid-Cheshire's public rights of way since 1961. It was formed to bring together people who enjoy walking and who are interested in keeping open and well-signed the public rights of way in an area stretching roughly from Runcorn and Warrington in the north to the Shropshire border in the south and from the M6 motorway in the east to the Welsh border in the west. Its objectives also include the preservation and enhancement of the beauty of the countryside for the benefit of the public as well as the development and maintenance of a network of well-defined public footpaths for local and visitor use.

The Society works closely with the Cheshire County Council's Public Rights of Way Unit and whenever and wherever possible in cooperation with landowners and their tenants in order to maintain the public's right to use footpaths and bridleways while respecting the legitimate needs of those who live and work in the countryside, especially the farming community. We walk the paths, carry out minor maintenance, report to the County Council on the condition of the paths and work with them to address problems arising. We also waymark the paths on behalf of the County Council.

The Society conducts walks every Wednesday and on alternate Sundays led by our own experienced walk leaders. Guests are always welcome to "give us a try" and new members are, of course, particularly welcome!

We have also over the years developed a number of medium- and long-distance footpaths in the county to encourage the public to experience the interest and beauty that is on offer – for free! – while contributing to a healthy lifestyle. At the time of writing these paths are:

Baker Way – 22 km (14 miles) from Chester station to Linmere in Delamere Forest.

Delamere Way – 34 km (21 miles) from Frodsham via Delamere Forest to Stockton Heath near Warrington.

Eddisbury Way – 26 km (18 miles) from Frodsham to the Sandstone Trail at Burwardsley.

Longster Trail – 15 km (10 miles) from Chester to Helsby Hill.

South Cheshire Way – 55 km (35 miles) from Mow Cop to Grindley Brook near Whitchurch.

All of these routes are shown on the OS "Explorer" maps. To these we can now add:

North Cheshire Way – 114 km (71 miles) from Hooton (Wirral) to Disley near Stockport, with a spur from Chester to Croughton.

Booklets are available from the Society for all of these walks except the North Cheshire Way – where you are already even better informed by your purchase of this book! Further details of the Society and its walks are available on its own web site at: http://www.mcfs.org.uk

Acknowledgments

The Mid-Cheshire Footpath Society is most grateful to the following organisations that have variously provided support, encouragement and/or financial assistance towards the development of the North Cheshire Way and the publication of this guide:

Cheshire County Council – for a generous grant, assistance in planning the route, the provision of valuable information for this guide and the waymarks that we have erected to sign the route.

Cheshire Rambling and Hill Walking Club (in memory of David Kinsell)

FH Properties Ltd. (Frank Hockenhull and David Vernon)

Macclesfield Borough Council

Mersey Forest, supported by Linley, Wightman, Shaw Foundation

Peak & Northern Footpaths Society

Ramblers' Association (Merseyside and West Cheshire Area)

Vale Royal Borough Council

Photographs: The following photographs (copyright holder's name in parenthesis) are used under a Creative Commons licence: p15 Lyme Park and p102 (Alan Fleming); p44 (Gary Rogers); p52 (David Crocker); p71 (Paul Baxter); p78 (Roger Gittins); p84 (Gary Barber); p85 (Peter Ward); p 93 (Stuart & Fiona Jackson). Permission to use the following photographs has been provided as indicated: p8 deer, squirrel and snail (J Savonen, Finland); p43 (Cheshire County Council). Those on p37 are from the internet and appear to be free of copyright in the UK. All of the other photographs in this book were provided by individual members of The Mid-Cheshire Footpath Society who retain the copyright thereto.

The members and Committee of the Society are especially grateful to David Kinsell – a long-term member of the Society, walker, musician and friend – who came up with the idea and was "godfather" to the North Cheshire Way from its inception. We are saddened that he did not live to see the completion of the project and dedicate this guide to his memory.

Walking the North Cheshire Way –
an alternative view

Are you *sure* this is the route?
(caves at Frodsham)

It *said* "go through the gate"
(copper mine at Alderley Edge)

Just thinking of the author ...
(stocks at Great Budworth)

I've had enough ...
(bus stop at Styal Country Park)